My Life as a White Belt

By Dan VanDetta

Author's Note:

I want to dedicate this, my first foray into the world of published literature, to my brother – Dylan VanDetta. I would neither be here, nor would I have had the opportunity to succeed as I have without his intervention, love, and support. Thank you, sir. You proved to me that life is worth living and that it only takes one person's caring to provide hope.

Foreword:

All of us in this existence, to some extent or another, must face trials and tribulations. My experiences have shown me that it is how we, as individuals, take on those challenges and recover from the blows that life can deliver that are the true measures of strength within us.

It is my sincere desire that the story of my journey can offer inspiration and motivation to those who may be able to relate, or at the very least some amusement to those who find it more difficult to do so.

All that I ask of you as a reader is to keep an open mind. Challenge yourself to ask questions like "What can I do to improve my life?" and "What are the moments in my past that are holding me back?" Questioning is the first step towards taking action.

I consider myself to have been a regular guy. I had many of the same ups and downs in life that many people experience. My capacity to handle adversity proved to be no greater than the 'Average Joe'. I failed to handle some of life's tougher experiences with even a modicum of grace. Alternatively, I persisted in some situations where many would have given up. Ultimately, I believe that you must be the judge when it comes to deciding whether or not your life is a success. Society, friends, and family may provide feedback or a framework for that decision, but it is within yourself that you will find the answers.

No longer do I consider myself average or regular or even 'normal'. I am exceptional. I am driven by passion and a fervor that no one and nothing can extinguish. I readily acknowledge that there is still a lot to learn and that there are many goals that I have yet to accomplish, but in this moment I love the person that I have become. I believe that I have the tools to shape my life into what I want it to be.

What follows is the story of how I became who I am now.

"Look not mournfully into the past, it comes not back again. Wisely improve the present, it is thine. Go forth to meet the shadowy future without fear and with a manly heart." – Henry Wadsworth Longfellow

The First Step:

The sign says 'All are welcome!' Does that mean me, too? I've spent almost two years trying to recover enough of my emotional, mental, and physical selves to feel human again. The divorce took more out of me than I thought possible, but it's definitely time to make some changes. I thought I'd figured out how to find myself again. Decent income, new relationship, stronger family ties; they all felt right for a while. Then the lady found greener pastures, a DUI crash and arrest set me back on my heels financially, and the family had its own set of issues to deal with. Almost back to square one, it seemed. So now I'm adapting to a new lifestyle without a vehicle and a part time job. I have few friends in the local area and am kind of clueless on how to find more. This place is right up the road... super convenient! I've got a background in wrestling, even if it was 20 years ago. Maybe this is a place I can take a risk on.

How will I fit in at Five Rings Jiu Jitsu Academy? Five Rings... is that related to the Olympics or something?! I hope they aren't super competitive. I can't handle that yet. I just want a place to get in shape and maybe learn some cool moves. All the jiu jitsu stuff I know is what I've seen on UFC fights. It would be awesome to know how to do arm bars and triangle chokes, even if I don't ever use them in real life. I started running back in August and I finally quit smoking again. I've even started biking all over the place. I should be able to handle this, no worries. Who knows... maybe I can show them a thing or two! Ha-ha!

Well, there's nothing left to do but open that door. I think the guy at the front desk might have noticed me pacing around out here. Man, this is nuts. What am I thinking? These guys all know each other already. They'll all be stronger, faster, and younger than me. I remember hearing that these jiu jitsu guys are kind of elitist. I don't need any condescension in my life right now. I'm going to check this place out on the internet and see if there are any reviews or if they have a website or something.

(...I walk down the hill to my apartment complex...)

Hmmm. I find nothing but good stuff online. Website is informative and they've got this free trial deal. It seems like there isn't much to lose. I am signing up for an orientation tomorrow. I'll see where this goes, I guess.

Orientation:

The tall guy at the desk introduces himself – Eric; seems to be about my age, but in a heck of a lot better shape than I am. Fairly sure he could kick my ass. He is a super friendly dude, though. He asks me how I heard about Five Rings and after I tell him my situation he gives me a tour of the facility. It turns out that they have fitness programs as well as jiu jitsu classes, which is awesome because I just cancelled my membership at my gym when I moved. Maybe I can work out up here, too. He tells me that there is a 'BJJ 1' class starting in a little while and that if I want to participate I can borrow a VIP gi and get started. No time like the present, since I am already here, right? Eric gets me the gi and shows me the locker room. It is a pretty sweet set up, with showers and plenty of storage space. No locks or lockers, though – this definitely isn't Los Angeles anymore.

Coach Nick isn't exactly what I have in mind when I think about martial arts instructors. He's patient, unassuming, and even a little goofy! Most importantly, he really seems to know his stuff. This class is fun – I am getting to learn some real basics of the sport, but even better I am witnessing the atmosphere at the gym. A higher level class is going on at the same time and the techniques that they are doing are really exciting. Everybody seems focused, but laid back at the same time. I am definitely going to ride this free trial out... I worked up a sweat from just rolling around a bit. Coach even said he could tell that I had wrestled before, which is cool because I didn't mention it.

I stick around to watch the other class finish. Nothing that they are doing seems that difficult. For certain, I can do that stuff without too many problems. There are people of all shapes and sizes; men, women, young, old. I swear I just saw that 120-pound girl just reverse positions on a guy fifty pounds heavier. The belt/rank system is a little confusing. There are white, blue, and purple belts in the class I am watching and it is being led by a guy about my age and size with a black belt. Why would they have them all in one class? Maybe they let the higher belts come in to help the lower ones? That would be sweet! When I was teaching, I used to do that with my more advanced students. Peer education is a solid teaching tool. Anyhow, I am also noticing that there is a progression between the instructor talking and the students practicing that should work well for me. I don't want to sit and listen to theory about the magic power of jiu jitsu for an hour, but I also don't want to get thrown to the wolves and get beat up for an hour either. Explain and practice is about the best I can hope for, I think. Hmm, think I'll explore a little bit.

This Pro Shop they have has some wicked apparel. T-shirts, patches, full gis, rash guards... all emblazoned with various logos. As I'm checking it out, Eric comes over and tells me about some of the items, including the Jiu Jitsu University book. I guess it's kind of like the gym handbook or something. It sounds interesting, even if I've never heard of this Saulo Ribeiro guy. I probably won't buy it though. I am here to work up a sweat and maybe meet some new people. Overall, I think this place has some possibilities. There are open, welcoming people who seem to enjoy what they are doing. Jiu jitsu is close enough to wrestling that I don't feel completely out of my depth, even if lying flat on my back is a little weird. I am really looking forward to my next class.

Initiation:

Today I try the fitness class for the first time. It's being instructed by Jessica, who reminds me of someone I once knew and as with just about everyone else here looks like she could kick my ass. I remember seeing her in the upper level jiu jitsu class, too. A blue belt, if memory serves. There are quite a few other folks in this fitness group and after some brief introductions we get started.

"Glute" bridges, overhead pulls, cats and dogs, opposite hand/leg raises, active clocks, one-legged side leans, kneeling groins; it's like I'm learning a new language. We're stretching a lot and there is a lot of focus on correct technique. It seems that I currently suck at stretching, but at least the feedback is constructive and not critical. The biggest issue I am facing is that I am already getting tired and only twenty minutes have gone by! What did I get myself into? No one else seems to be having any trouble – especially Patricia. She's an older lady, but damn is she fit. Mental note: Try to keep up with Patricia.

Okay, now we're getting to the meat of the workout – lots of pushing and pulling – T-stand push-ups, TRX rows, multiplanar dumbbell raises, and renegade rows – more new terminology and this time they hurt! Trying my best to keep a good face on things, but my muscles and lungs are already blown. I did not pace myself well. Argh! Breathe, Dan, breathe… just do what you can. No one is giving you a hard time and there's no prize at the end of class. Slow and steady wins the race.

Jessica transitions us into the conditioning portion of the class. Wait… what?!? You mean that wasn't just conditioning we were doing??? I look at the clock for the umpteenth time. Still fifteen minutes left… I can do this. Where the hell is my cardio? I run close to 3 miles at least every other day! I guess those seventeen years of smoking are still affecting me. Bah! No excuses! Push through the pain! Rapid response drill, bear crawls, roller coasters, Aerodynes (bikes), and d-ball slams add up to happy, fun, torture time.

When the time runs out on the last exercise I am exhausted, but energized. It's been too long since I pushed myself that hard. Having someone there to support, educate, and cheer me on is just what I need to get back into shape, because tonight showed me just how far I have to go. But I made it! Hopefully I won't be too sore tomorrow! Jessica high-fives everyone and welcomes me to come back for more.

So far, so good.

Continuation:

Coach Nick has decided that I am ready to move up to the BJJ 2 + 3 class. Sounds good to me! From what I have seen, they do some cool stuff and get to spar with each other. The first difference is warm-ups. Lizard crawls? Ugh, my hips are all tight and 'crunchy'. Not used to this kind of stretching. And don't get me started on these pendulum drills. I feel like a fish flopping around on the mat. On top of that, I am already winded! I watch the other people in class and the blue belts flow around their partner's legs like it is second nature. The other new folks are struggling to varying degrees just like I am, so that gives me a little perspective. I am reminded of wrestling practice; we used to have all sorts of funky (and fun!) warm-ups. I'm sure that before long I will get better at these.

I got this cool gi in my introductory package, but I must need to break it in or something. It's a little stiff and it is scraping the heck out of my skin. Maybe I will get one of those rash guards they sell in the shop. I'm also sweating like crazy. I've always perspired a lot, but this is ridiculous. I feel like a water sprinkler. Who's going to want to roll with me? One gi isn't going to cut it. It's only been a couple of classes and the sleeves on this one are already getting ugly. That's something to worry about later though. Coach Tom is ready to start class.

So I've met Tom Oberhue a couple of times since starting up here. Friendly, welcoming, professional – these adjectives come easily to mind when I think of him. Turns out I can add corny to that list! Man, these jokes are such groaners. And that laugh! Love it! Ha-ha. Aside from that, we get down to business. He explains that we'll be working on something called cross sides bottom this week and demonstrates how to get to your edge, zero position (protecting your top arm from getting under hooked and using your bottom hand to protect from a cross face), and two ways to improve your position (shooting your leg through to quarters position or recovering guard). We watch the demonstration, then he answers some technical questions, and then we try it out. I have to stop myself from asking questions. It's always been a habit of mine to overanalyze material before I try it. I definitely don't want to fall into that pattern here. I don't have a partner, but it sorts itself out fairly quickly as people pair off.

I end up with a younger guy with a blue belt who introduces himself as Robert. He was also the guy that Coach Tom used as a partner for demonstration so I assume he knows what he's doing. Turns out he does! He walks me through the moves because even though I was paying attention it is more complex than I thought. The movements are really foreign to me. I have to get used to being on my back and on my side with my back angled toward the mat. Not to mention, I haven't done any kind of contact sport in well over a decade. I can tell already that I am using muscles that I haven't used in a long, long time.

Coach periodically provides feedback as we're drilling. I notice that he makes an effort to help everyone, not just the higher belts. In fact, everyone is communicating a lot. I hear partners sharing constructive information on each other's moves on a regular basis. This bodes well for the future, I think. We come back together to fine tune some parts of the cross sides position. Then we go back and work it a little bit more. My hip flexors are really bugging me now, particularly when I shoot my leg back to try to get to quarters position. I ask Robert about it and he suggests that I talk to Coach Eric in my next class. It turns out that Eric is a coach and a licensed massage therapist. I make a mental note to catch up with him soon.

Next, we get a chance to practice what we've learned in something called positional sparring. Coach Tom explains that the drill is for 'Simon' and that the other partner (Garfunkel) should only provide a percentage of resistance. Ha! Simon and Garfunkel! Coach is definitely from my generation. Anyhow, we get to it. I try my best, and I have some success surviving from the bottom position. I don't do so well on top. Robert keeps escaping, so I go harder and try to press him into the mat using what I remember from wrestling. Coach notices and reminds me that this isn't a full spar and that to be a good partner I need to give different levels of resistance at different times. *boggle*. You mean I'm not supposed to try to win when we do this? I don't get it. I can tell that I'm a little stronger than Robert and I outweigh him by 25 pounds at least. Not sure my ego will let me just let him beat me. Of course, I'm breathing like a forge bellows and he's acting like it's a walk in the park but still I should get the best of it, right? I'm still confused by this as we come back together to end class.

Coach Tom gives some announcements about upcoming events. This guy named Jeff Glover is coming to do a seminar. That sounds cool. There is a tournament about 2 months away. I am so not ready for that though. We bring our hands together and on two we yell 'Five Rings!' then bump knuckles in a circle. I get turned around to the general amusement of the class, but finally get straightened out. Everyone is very welcoming and introduces themselves. Even with the confusion, this was a fun class. I am beat, though. Time to hit the sack and hope I am not too sore in the morning.

Immersion:

Whew... this is my fifth class this week, if you count fitness. I think I can officially say that I am hooked. This sport, facility, and community are exactly what I needed. I can't remember the last time I felt quite so motivated to move forward and make progress towards a goal. Well, that's not true. I can remember the last few times pretty clearly, but the circumstances then were on the negative end of the spectrum. It was a little under two years ago that I was living in my car, struggling to find meaning in a life that didn't make sense to me anymore. Poor decision after poor judgment call led to a spiral of intense self-destruction. It seems so long ago some days and like only yesterday on others.

Today, right now, this very moment it couldn't feel farther away if it were eons ago – I'm applying a choke that I just learned from back with hooks. Bow and arrow choke, I believe it's called. I'm not very good at it yet, but it is extremely empowering to know that I hold someone's consciousness in my hands. This whole jiu jitsu thing is full of moments just like this one. Empowering, humbling, exciting! I think I've even developed an affinity for getting choked out (well, almost anyhow). Hmm, does that mean I'm odd? That moment of fuzziness right before you go out is so peaceful. It's like there's this panic and then you stop caring. I'm sure there's a medical phenomenon associated with it, but I don't care to do that much research. Anyhow, this choke is cool and all but as I said I am struggling with how to position my body to finish it effectively. Coach has expressed several times that drilling on our own is the best way to commit something to muscle memory. I find that when I come in to open mat time it is hard to get away from sparring – I think because it is so much fun to rough house a little and try out the things you've learned from the previous week. I know it is important to drill, though.

This guy I met last week has been helping me stay focused on my goals and how to accomplish them. His name is Bruce, and he's been participating in the sport for a while now. He is still a white belt, but with a few stripes to his credit. I dig his approach; he keeps a journal where he writes down moves and techniques that we've learned and he likes to methodically go over and drill the moves so that they get committed to muscle memory. He's got a couple nagging injuries, which I can relate to at this point, so we take it easy on the full out sparring and concentrate on honing the technique. We also take some time to chat and get to know each other a bit. He confirms what I've already discovered, which is that even though the people here come from such varied backgrounds there always seems to be some connecting experience that makes it easy to communicate on some level.

Don't get me wrong, this isn't some utopian commune where everyone is a super amazing human being; I've met a handful that rub me the wrong way for one reason or another. But the more I come here, the more I feel myself changing. I'm more open and more forgiving, of myself and others. The more I train, the better I feel about myself. I think that is why I find myself altering my schedule to make time to be up here. Fifth class this week, and I may just try to get a couple more in. That tournament in March is starting to sound mighty interesting!

Injury:

Tuesday night after BJJ 2 + 3 class the gym runs this class called tournament rounds. It's technically a BJJ 4 class, but I have noticed that several white belts attend on a regular basis. So I decide to give it a shot. Coach Tom separates us on the mat from big to bigger to biggest. I hang out in the bigger section and hope to find some other white belts to roll with. The blues and higher intimidate the hell out of me still. Okay, if I am being honest, it is my ego that tends to avoid them. My limited experience has shown me that I am able to make very little headway against them. We start off with some positional sparring and I have some success and some failure, but more than anything I realize how much I can learn from these things. Gaps in my game flash like neon signs in front of me.

I spot this hardcore looking guy that I haven't seen at the gym before. Shaved head, tattoos — turns out to be one of the many Nicks at the gym (definitely the most common first name!). We roll and it becomes evident that we're fairly evenly matched. Both of us ramp things up until we're going after each other pretty intensely. I get an Americana on him, but can't finish it because he's Gumby's cousin. He reverses me and gets a body triangle from the back. Straining, breathing, struggling… POP. He submits me with a rear naked choke and we disentangle ourselves. Something isn't quite right, but it's time to move on to the next partner. My conditioning still isn't up to snuff and I was already wheezing like a wildebeest after a stampede before the last roll. Now every inhalation brings a sharp pain in my ribcage. I continue to roll until I just can't take the pain anymore. I head home without mentioning it to anyone.

It's hard to sleep. Every time I roll over or try to breathe deeply I get that sharp pain. I toss back a couple of ibuprofen and try to make the best of it. I have to ask myself what it is exactly that I'm trying to accomplish. What if I broke a rib or something serious? I don't have health insurance at the moment and a major injury would pretty much redefine my life in a very negative way. Am I pushing too hard? Trying to do too much too soon? I need to talk to the coaches and see what they advise.

(...one fitful night of sleep later...)

Coach Eric and Coach Tom tell me that what has most likely happened is that I popped a rib through some cartilage, and while it can certainly be annoying if I am careful I can continue to slow roll. The key is getting enough rest and communicating well with my partners. I can manage that. I do *not* want to stop training. I'm learning so much and having so much fun. This is an eye-opener though. I'm not twenty-five anymore and this isn't going to heal in a couple of days. I need to understand my body's limits and pace myself accordingly. One of the things that Coach Tom tells me really sticks in my brain: "You've started a journey, Dan, and it isn't a race. A black belt is a white belt that didn't quit."

Well, I'm not quitting. I am going to be smarter about this, though.

Absolution:

Recovery is as slow as I expected. I've had to tell my training partners to watch out for my ribs and not to put too much pressure on me when we're rolling. I forget once and Coach Nick demonstrates the knee-to-belly position on me. The scream that escapes from me is similar to that of a small child when they stub their toe on a rock. That, I am informed, is an example of a 'verbal' tap out. The combination of Coach's chagrin and my shameful scream is enough for me to never forget to communicate thoroughly about injuries again.

One of the things that I notice is that despite the inherently violent nature of jiu jitsu (the goals of the sport include choking someone unconscious or bending their joints until they give up), very few of the practitioners enjoy inflicting pain. In Coach Nick's case, he's actually pretty worked up that he hurt me. I reassure him that it was my responsibility, but I can tell that he is upset. I promise him that I will do better at informing my partners of my infirmity and this seems to mollify him to a certain degree.

I spent far too much of my life trying to hide things about myself. Things that I thought would diminish me in the eyes of others – like, for instance, when I would be injured or sick. I was so concerned that others would think me unreliable or incapable that I would lie to them and even to myself in order to save face. I am starting to see now that I did myself and my friends, colleagues, and family a disservice with this dishonesty. This situation with my coach is not an example of deliberate dissembling, but it still highlights the effects of poor communication with those who rely on you or that you rely on or care about. I vow to own this and not make the same mistake twice.

An extremely beneficial side effect of my injury is that it slows me down. I am forced to use the techniques we are learning because my strength has been sapped and my speed has been hamstrung. A whole new side of training is revealing itself as I start to understand that I'm doing more than just working out and building up a sweat when I come to class. I am learning a foundation that is fundamental to progress in jiu jitsu. The intricacy of what I thought was a very simplistic move (the double leg smash pass) start to become understandable when I have to slow it down and really think about them. Coach Tom's references to applied power through the use of technique start to make sense.

I do believe my game is changing. So is how I look at myself. No more lies. It takes more than words to make something true. Walk the walk, Dan.

Oh, and I also need to buy a bike. Riding the bus everywhere is getting old fast. Court date for my DUI is coming up soon.

Illumination:

I spend a lot more time observing others than I used to. Overall, I've been a pretty self-centered guy for the majority of my life. Now I feel like I am able to watch what others are doing and really am aware of what's going on. Take this drill we're doing as an example: the Lovato flow is what Coach Eric calls it. I am watching it being demonstrated and I am starting to understand how the transitions and positioning allow the arm bar at the end of the flow to become a reality for the person performing it. Then, I am able to apply what I've seen and put it into practice in my own drills.

I'm starting to understand that there is a connection here, if I can only make it. There are some people in this community that I can really learn from, and not just jiu jitsu moves. There are successful businesspeople, folks in healthy relationships, and individuals with productive goals that they have realistic ways of reaching. Maybe if I hang around long enough I can figure out how to do these things for myself. I definitely need a new road map for life. The last one had too many pit-stops in hell.

The famous names of jiu jitsu get tossed around the gym a lot – Saulo and Xande Ribeiro, Rafael Lovato, the Gracies... I don't have a ton of familiarity with these guys, but I get the impression that they've earned their reputations. Another name that is a little newer on the scene is Jeff Glover. Known for his dynamic and innovative style, he's had some recent success at big tournaments. Five Rings gets him to come and do a seminar for us. As I meet him and listen to his insights on this sport that I'm growing to love, I feel like I'm in the presence of someone who gets it. His game seems more applicable to smaller athletes, but one thing I take away is how he moves his hips. Everything evolves from his hip positioning. Not to mention that he could be an acrobat – I've never seen anyone use a stability ball like he does.

Hip movement, observation, application – things are starting to fall into place. I just have to keep at this. Regular attendance, continued sobriety, and focus should be all I need to stay on track. My DUI hearing ended up turning out about as well as I could have hoped. Minimum fine, lots of community service, victim's panel, and a year- long license suspension. Bike is moving up the priority list. Oh, and another source of income. Not subbing is killing my budget. I am still able to make it to a couple of gigs a month, but that just isn't cutting it.

Running and fitness are making some significant changes on my body, too. I've already lost about eight pounds since I started at Five Rings. I'm going to do something I swore I would never do as well. I'm going to start looking at my diet and maybe make some changes. Gasp!

Promotion:

As I walk up to the gym for the third time today, I start to realize that this is becoming a lifestyle. Not a hobby or casual athletic workout, but a significant shift in my habits and activity level. Every day I wake up I am starting to feel a little healthier, a little more energetic. Don't get me wrong, I still feel like I have a long way to go on my journey, but it is nice to be able to recognize the growth. I've always thrived on tangible achievement.

It seems like nothing much is different tonight: we warm up and do our drills and work on our technique. Coach Tom is cracking jokes and making references to things that only those of us in the 35+ crowd have any hope of understanding. We build up a sweat, help each other learn, and try to piece together our jiu jitsu puzzle. Another day at the office... if you're lucky enough to have your office be an adult playground where you get to roll around with your friends for an hour and a half at a time.

At the end of class, Coach goes to a back room and comes back with some pieces of tape hanging from a pirouette bar, some black and some white. He explains that promotions at Five Rings are meant to mark growth and learning and progress along your path. I look around the room and try to guess who could be getting promoted. Maybe Robert is getting a stripe on his blue belt – he's so technical and basically lives at the gym. Or it could be Nick (one of the five, this one is the tall blue belt). His game is so unique and his work ethic is admirable. I realize I have no idea what it really takes to get a stripe or a new belt.

Coach continues by stating that belting does not represent branding at Five Rings. There is no test to take or extra fee that you have to pay to advance, like I've heard that some gyms do. That's nice to hear, but I have to admit that even at this point I can't imagine switching gyms or training regularly somewhere else. It already feels like home. They don't have to compel my loyalty. It is freely given.

Finally, Coach calls out some names... not Robert or Nick this time, but several of my white belt training partners are called up for 2nd, 3rd, or 4th stripes. Lo and behold, my name is also called. My first stripe! I don't know how to react so I numbly walk up and bow and shake hands with Coach Tom and Coach Eric. They say it is well deserved. I wonder how that can be. Sure, I spend a lot of time up here but I feel like I have so much more to learn. Well, they are the coaches and who am I to doubt their judgment? I accept the stripe proudly, ready to take on the challenges that will lead me to the next one.

Preparation:

Trap the forearm with the same side hand, and then grab the triceps with the opposite hand with palm facing away and pinky towards the ceiling – Hand Position #1. This position is particularly effective for attacking from the closed guard. Transitions from a pit stop position to an arm bar or triangle submission are possible evolutions of the hand position.

When I think about this, analyze it, take it apart and put it back together it makes more and more sense. It's a recipe! Step by step instructions to get from point A to point B. Sure, there are other possibilities along the way; branches off the road to get to different destinations. But the most direct line is available by following simple, easy-to-remember directions. How many times have I overcomplicated things in my life by not just doing what made the most sense? This makes sense, so I am not going to question it. I'm just going to do it. And do it again. Until it comes so naturally that I don't even have to think about it.

Translation for life outside the gym: Get up. Establish a healthy routine. Avoid complications. Remove stressors. Face the world with an open mind and an open heart. Build relationships with positive people. Set goals and accomplish them. Get plenty of sleep. Do it again. This makes sense.

There is a tournament up near Seattle coming up fairly soon called the Revolution. Still not sure if I am ready for that yet, but I want to challenge myself. I'm getting better at some things. My conditioning is improving by leaps and bounds. Between fitness classes and jiu jitsu training I am now spending close to 15 hours a week at the gym. And having a blast doing it! It seems to be a logical next step to add a competitive endeavor to my list of goals.

Tournament preparation at the gym is intense, but full of constructive feedback. There is a 'fine-tuning' aspect that I really like –

taking the things you know and making them better and more efficient as opposed to piling on as many new moves as possible. I feel myself getting excited at the prospect of testing out what I've learned against someone else. I express my interest to the coaches and they encourage me to register.

I have to stop and ask myself if this is too much, too soon. Can I handle the frustration of training competitively and the possible disappointment of losing after all that training? I realize that if I don't test myself then I will just end up treading water safely in the shallow end of the pool. Life is full of risks. There are lots of people who hide in their safe little worlds without taking any chances. I'm not interested in being those people. Look out, Revolution – here I come!

Tournament:

It can be a long drive from Portland to Seattle. That is, if you aren't packed into a car with people like Robert, Louisa, and Justin. I haven't laughed this hard in a long time, whether it's at Justin's singing or Louisa's making fun of Robert's driving or Robert's driving itself. The laughter is to some extent an extension of the nervous energy we all feel; that electricity that you feel before going to battle. The Revolution tournament looms on the horizon and we're all excited, apprehensive, and ready to show what we've learned.

Coach Tom often uses the expression 'Oss!' I did a little research and found out the following:

One definition of "Oss", also known as "ossu", means Oshi Shinobu, which conveys the idea of "persevering when pushed", or in other words, never give up, have determination, grit and withstand the most arduous of training. Carrying on without giving up, under all kinds of pressure - that's the idea of inner strength so common in Asian culture.

This concept is one that I have unknowingly been familiar with for a long time, just by other labels. And as I approach the forthcoming combat I re-examine periods of my life where I have had to persevere when pushed. Growing up without a mother and father, there are many times when I wanted to give up. I had to find other sources of guidance – my big brothers, my grandparents, coaches, teachers. There were days when every moment felt like stepping on the mat to take on a new challenger. I was forced to dig deep or be overwhelmed by the stressors in my life. I found comfort in the routine – sports practices and competitions, school work, extracurricular clubs, reading – anything that helped me feel stable.

Later on in life, I lost touch with those routines. Partying, drinking, smoking, drug use – these became more the norm. I no longer had the resources to persist when pushed. I'd managed to alienate so much of my support network that I felt very alone and incapable of doing things that needed to be done to survive, much less thrive.

Things are different now... as we pull up to the hotel, I realize that while those days are not so far gone I once again have family and friends to rely on; solid training to use as a resource in my fight; coaches and teammates to support and uplift me. Now all I need is a good night's rest and I will be ready for anything.

(*Insert a restless night of enduring Justin's snoring...*)

The high school gym is abuzz with anticipation. I see the familiar faces of my coaches and the Five Rings crew arrives and prepares our area in the bleachers. Proudly displaying our banner and blowing the vuvuzelas, this part of the Ribeiro family is ready to compete. I have some of the first matches of the day so I check my brackets to see who I will be going up against. There are three other guys in my division, so the most matches I can get is two. This is probably a good thing, considering my conditioning is still not top notch. I realize fairly quickly that seeing a name means essentially nothing so I decide to focus on going over my game plan and staying loose. I wanted to ease into the competitive aspect of jiu jitsu so I tried to make things as easy on myself as possible – I registered in a comfortable weight class and in the master's division so I will be competing with guys approximately my age. Hopefully it pays off with a good experience!

Almost time to rock n' roll! I see some guys getting ready to weigh in who look to be in my division. They aren't particularly intimidating, but then I don't imagine that I am either. Thirty-seven years old, 185 pounds, one stripe on my belt – yeah, I am not striking fear into anyone's heart. It's hard to stay warmed-up in a breezy high school hallway while waiting around for what seems like hours, but is more likely thirty minutes or so. As we step into the weighing area, I feel that electricity again. I've even got goose bumps. Anticipation builds, my first match awaits. I. Am. Ready.

Tournament (cont.) –

Respect is a concept that has always been a struggle for me. I was told from a young age that I needed to respect my elders, well, just because I was supposed to. My adolescent brain struggled with the concept of 'earned' respect because I saw a lot of contradictions in my life – some people seemed to get respect for no obvious reason, while others who worked hard and had integrity didn't get as much as I thought they should. Over time, the concept became clearer for me as it pertained to others, but I still had difficulty when it came to applying it to me.

As I step on the mat something becomes crystal clear to me. This guy facing me has no reason to respect me. We've never met. He has no idea what I've been through or how hard I've trained. If I want his respect I am going to have to *take* it from him. I have to show him – right here, right now – that if he wants this victory it will be by going through my best effort. And so it begins...

He pulls guard immediately and begins to attack. I feel the adrenaline pump through my veins as I establish posture and try to open his defenses. I block an arm bar attempt, a triangle, an omaplata; he has a strong bottom game. I finally get his guard opened and sprawl on the nearside leg. Quick bounce, fast feet, and I get the pass. I work directly into the only real submission I know at this point: a claw choke that we've practiced over the last couple of weeks. My technique is solid right up until the finishing point, but I can't close the deal. I hear him gurgle a tad, but it just isn't enough.

My heart and mind are racing. My breath comes in deep pulls, desperately trying to get more oxygen to my lungs. He escapes and recovers guard. Back and forth we go until he sinks in a triangle attempt. I recognize it early and my body takes over – stack, posture up, rotate. I crash down and smash pass into mount. Now I've got him! I start to attack his lapels and before I know it I am the one on my back. I got cocky and now I'm defending from the bottom. There is a pause in the action as we both take stock of our new positions and try to muster some energy.

My coach, Aaron, gives words of encouragement. "Breathe, Dan! Relax. You're doing great!" I think I've spoken to Aaron once before this match, but he is a higher belt and really knows jiu jitsu. His presence bolsters my flagging reserves and I prepare to defend myself. My opponent tries to stand up in guard against me, so I grab his ankle and sweep him to mount! Six points! I am well ahead at this time, but I don't dare slack off. I have no idea how much time has gone by. It feels like an eternity. My lungs are burning. My forearms ache from over gripping. Suddenly, it's over. Time is called. My first five minutes of competition have passed.

Victory is sweet, but even more valued is that elusive sense of respect. From my opponent, from my teammates and coaches, and from myself. I earned this! I realize, too, that my respect for my adversary is great and I congratulate him on a hard fought match. My elation at winning is short lived, as my coach informs me that I have only a short time before I must test my will once more. My aches and pains and fatigue come to the forefront of my consciousness.

Again? Okay. Here we go. One more time.

Frustration:

If you've ever seen a bulldog in a fight with another animal then you are probably familiar with the incredible amount of damage they can take while putting themselves in a position to lock their teeth onto their prey's skin and work their way up into a killing position. Even if you haven't, you can probably imagine the amount of perseverance and fortitude it must take for them to accomplish their goal. This is not a tale of perseverance and fortitude. This is what it is like to be on the other side of that locked jaw.

I step out onto the mat with forearms still burning from my first match. I had over gripped and now I was paying the price. I had watched my upcoming opponent dismantle his adversary in his first match. It might have taken him forty seconds or so. Even so, I feel like I am faster than him and should be able to use the techniques I've learned to overcome his advantages.

These concerns fly out of my brain as we touch hands and begin our battle. We latch onto each other in the classic fifty/fifty grip – my right hand on his left lapel and left hand on his right sleeve; him with the same on me. We test each other mightily, throwing our bodies around the mat with neither of us gaining much advantage. His grips are like iron! Even two on one I have a difficult time forcing him to release my lapel. He seizes an opening and tries to throw me using a **seoi nage** – one of the few judo techniques I've actually learned to defend up to this point. I drop my center of gravity as he tries to pull me over and I am able to duck under his arm and get to side control.

My lack of experience begins to shine through at this point. He quickly snags one of my legs with his and draws me into half guard while pulling one of my sleeves across my body. Before I know it, he is taking my back! I protect my neck and try everything I know how to escape. I peel his hands from my collar and try to drive under his hooks to no avail. Precious seconds tick by. Coach Aaron keeps me updated on the score, so I am well aware that I am behind. I must find a way to get him off my back. Every time I succeed in pulling one of his limbs away and creating some daylight, another one slips in to slam the door.

Thirty seconds left – I dig deep for any reserve of energy hidden within. I find nothing. My arms are dead. My breathing is labored and hampered even more by the fact that my opponent now has me face-down on the mat, still with his legs laced around mine and driving his hips into the base of my lungs. Ten, nine, eight, seven... I struggle feebly as time expires. Defeat.

I lie on the mat with eyes closed and wonder what I did wrong. My opponent helps me to my feet and congratulates me on a good contest, much like I had done for my previous foe. I am disappointed. Frustrated. I worked hard and came up short of my ultimate goal. As they raise the other man's hand, my coach tells me about the good things that I had done; a bit hard to swallow, but I am grateful for the lack of criticism at this point.

My thoughts drift for a moment to my stepsons. I remember very clearly the day I left them. It seemed like the only way I could escape the drama that their mother was bringing to my door on an almost daily basis was to get far away. I was unhealthy and needed a respite, but it meant leaving them behind. On that day I felt more defeated and frustrated than I have ever felt in my entire life... including right now. This pales in comparison, but it gives me another chance to face a challenge and get through it. I still feel like I failed my boys, but that doesn't mean that I have to give in every time something gets hard. Life is hard, sometimes. It is how we handle adversity that is the true measure of our spirit, our humanity.

My teammates and coaches congratulate me on my silver medal and use kind words to bring my chin up. I resolve in this moment to train harder, learn as quickly as I can, and know that the next time I step on the mat for competition that I have no excuses for losing. For now though, I have a long car ride back to Portland to think about failure and stifled goals. Next time, things will be different.

Demarcation:

I've increased my training time to two to three fitness classes and four to five jiu jitsu classes per week. The benefits are readily apparent, as my conditioning and strength continue to improve. My technique is still clunky, but I also see improvements there. Trying to fit runs in at least three times a week, but that is a bit more hit and miss. The diet continues to improve – eating a lot more vegetables and cutting out sweets and snacks.

All of this coincides with my continued attendance at drug and alcohol treatment therapy and Alcoholics Anonymous meetings. I've been doing my community service at a place called Free Geek, where I've been building computers for those in need. Slowly, but surely, life seems to be coming back to a place where I feel settled. I have a routine that works. I seem to be making good choices and prioritizing correctly.

Coach Tom and Coach Eric have given me some new things to think about since the tournament. First and foremost is that there is still a ton of jiu jitsu that I haven't even been exposed to yet. So much so that there are basic, fundamental building blocks that aren't in place yet. I work hard to fill in those gaps. I drill the moves we learn in class at open mats. I watch YouTube videos of things I don't really understand yet and want to know more about. Next, I start working on finding out what is wrong with my hips. I have been in almost constant pain for weeks... no, make those months. It's very difficult for me to do full squats and lateral lunges. This is impacting my ability to perform many of the moves properly. This is also frustrating me on an emotional level because I can tell that it is holding my progress back. I talk with Adam – a very knowledgeable fitness instructor at the gym – and he starts me on a program to help alleviate the issue.

I am having more success at tournament rounds, but still struggle to make it to the end. It occurs to me that something Coach Tom spoke about after the Revolution could apply here. When I mentioned my burning forearms he told me that I was over gripping. I was applying too much energy over too much time and it was sapping that particular part of my body. In other words, I need to figure out how to pace myself and recognize better when to explode and attack and when to rest and take stock of my situation. I am trying to give every partner at sparring rounds my full energy when I should be going at closer to 85 or 90 percent, as well as using the applied energy technique.

The epiphanies keep popping up and I feel enlightened each time one does. I don't remember feeling this sense of wonder at learning something new since college – I have really missed it. Nose back to the grindstone... not the most apt phrase, perhaps, because no work I've ever done was this much fun!

Rehabilitation:

I've always had a bit of an irrational block against massage therapy, so I've never tried it. Couldn't really tell you why. Like I said, irrational. After talking with Adam (fitness coach) and several other gym members who swear it was extremely beneficial for them, I break down and schedule a session with Coach Eric, who is also a licensed massage therapist.

At this point, Eric has become more than just a coach for me. I've had the opportunity to get to know his family and visit his home to watch some UFC fights. The social outlets that he's included me in have helped me to start building healthy relationships with some truly excellent people, himself included. I also find myself admiring his approach to life – he's generally upbeat and takes adversity in stride. He also treats people with respect and therefore receives quite a bit from the entire gym community. Not a bad role model for someone trying to rebuild his life.

I fill out the form describing what's bothering me – namely my hip flexors and lower back. It's now at the point where I'm in constant pain whenever I am doing anything remotely active. I wake up sore and go to bed sore. It isn't sharp, stabbing agony. More like a dull throb that doesn't go away. I am seriously considering taking a long break to see if that helps to solve the problem. I really don't want to though. Despite the pain, my time at the gym is my favorite time of the day. I learn something new every class and I have a lot of acquaintances here now. Hopefully, Eric can help me out!

He is professional and friendly as we start the session, asking questions to determine exactly what needs to be done and walking me through the process since this is the first time I've done anything like this. I am surprised at how nervous I am. I really want the pain to end and to be able to have a full range of motion again.

The preconceived notions I had about what a massage is supposed to be like are quickly dashed from my thoughts. Instead of a lot of pounding and rubbing like you see in the movies, Eric uses pressure. It is almost clinical, as opposed to being sloppy or intrusive. At the same time, he keeps me talking... about myself, about jiu jitsu, and about other common interests. As we talk, I discover that he and I have quite a few overlapping experiences. The specifics vary, but we've both been down some difficult roads in our lives. He continues to work out the kinks in my body, allowing me to dictate how much pressure he applies in accordance to my pain threshold. I also become more and more informed about the different muscles that are causing me to hurt. Eric seems to know his business inside and out. He can also tell that I haven't ever had professional massage work done before. It seems that my leg muscles are particularly tight and unmoving.

Before I know it, the session is done. As I get down from the table I apprehensively put weight on my legs. A miracle! No more pain! I can do lateral lunges with a full range of motion!!! I want to do a jig, I'm so giddy. I give Eric a high-five and an enthusiastic 'Thank you!' This was so worth the money it cost. I can still sense that my body isn't completely happy, though. The great sensations throughout my hips and lower back seem to have highlighted the tightness I was unaware of before in other parts of my body, particularly my shoulders and neck. Well, they aren't painful at least... just a little tight. I'm guessing Eric can probably help with that, too. I am definitely scheduling another session with him.

As I settle up the bill and walk out the door, I realize that more important than a release from the pain I was feeling is that Eric is becoming my friend. Something I feel like I haven't had in quite a while... at least not someone I get to hang out with on a regular basis. It's a good revelation, and I walk home with a skip in my pain-free step and a lighter heart to accompany it.

Discovery:

Today we are getting a rare treat. Cadu Francis, one of our association's most accomplished black belts, is visiting to teach a session for Five Rings members. I have seen him on Xande's videos that play in an almost constant loop on the screen in the gym's front lobby so I know who to look for as I warm up on the mat. I remember joking with some teammates about how he has trouble focusing his eyes on one spot during the tapings. I realize that I probably won't share those jokes with him. He's a large man and has been a black belt for over nine years. As he enters with Coach Tom, I feel a thrill of anticipation for the coming lesson. I have really developed a love for this sport.

There are a lot of newer and unfamiliar faces here today. As for Jeff Glover, the big names of the sport seem to bring the folks from the morning, afternoon, and evening classes together. It's nice to see the community as a whole. Definitely makes me feel like part of an extended family. I see one of our purple belts and am reminded that I don't get along with every part of this new family.

I've only met him once before, but it was kind of humiliating. His cavalier attitude towards my inability to effectively roll with him hurt my feelings and I was too intimidated at the time to express that. Now I've harbored this resentment towards him and I don't know how to fix it. Ah, well, perhaps time will present me with an opportunity to do so. Patience is another personal attribute that I've been working on developing.

Cadu shows us a variety of warm-ups, which are interesting because it is my first experience with some of the more traditional jiu jitsu exercises and pre-workout routines. He then moves into a flow drill, a pass (not surprisingly dubbed the 'Cadu' pass), and a choke that I think is impressive, but that I am finding hard to implement. I can tell that he has put a lot of thought and reflection into his presentation. He makes a point to come around to each of us and offers tips on how to implement the techniques. My partner and I work through the moves and give each other feedback.

While this isn't the first time I've partnered with a female, this is definitely the first time I've worried about adjusting my intensity dial when rolling with one. Jessica and Lindsay are blue belts and seem to have a way of deflecting my heavier weight and redirecting my attacks so that my greater strength doesn't always work to my advantage. Liz, at first glance, seems to be a different story. If she weighs more than a buck twenty I'd eat my gi, which means she is spotting me a good sixty-five pounds or so. On top of that, she's relatively new to jiu jitsu. I am more than a little wary of hurting her by accident.

As the seminar progresses, it becomes readily apparent that my fear is unfounded and unnecessary. Liz is a beast! Along with the excellent lessons in jiu jitsu that I am getting from Cadu, I am also getting the unexpected bonus of one in humility. Her speed and surprising strength astonish me, and allow me to turn up the intensity dial to where it would normally be. This leads to some solid jiu jitsu 'conversation' (as Coach Tom likes to call it) and we are able to give each other good feedback. If I am not mistaken, from the way she moves Liz has a background in wrestling. I wonder if she competed in high school.

Cadu and Coach Tom wrap up the session and we have the opportunity to meet with our guest teacher. I get the opportunity to ask him about his jiu jitsu journey and I am struck by how humble his explanation is - "I am grateful for every day that I can step on the mat," he says. Powerful words that remain in my mind and cause me to reflect on what I learned today about assumptions and my preconceptions about women in my sport. Male, female, young, and old; there is an opportunity for everyone to succeed and thrive in the world of jiu jitsu. It also reminds me that the journey is too short for resentment. I'm going to approach that purple belt soon and clear the air. The journey is too short and I am not who I used to be.

Reflection:

I smoked cigarettes and drank alcohol for close to twenty years. I went through phases where I was drinking a two liter bottle of Pepsi and eating a box of fast food fried chicken for breakfast, then smoking the remainder of a pack of Marlboros for dinner. Shortly before starting on the path of jiu jitsu I had ballooned to two hundred fifteen pounds and had failed at my first attempt to quit smoking. I also felt a ton of anxiety over common stressors that others seemed to be able to take in stride. I battled depression on a daily basis.

I look at myself in the mirror these days and see myself transitioning to a much healthier place. I have lost close to twenty pounds in five months; my diet has greatly improved; I feel good about waking up in the morning. More than any of that, what makes me feel the greatest sense of accomplishment is that I can see how I am now able to set goals and achieve them. Whether it is on or off the mat, the things that I want for myself are slowly, but surely, coming to fruition. I have to stop once in a while and take stock of how this is happening.

Hard work? Check. I take care of my job responsibilities and do a little more than is required in order to stay in good standing with my employer. I am at the gym or on the road (running) whenever possible in order to improve my technique and conditioning. Perseverance? For certain. This process has been one of the most difficult things I've ever tried to do. I wake up sore and tired every day. I make next to nothing and go without whenever possible in order to maintain this lifestyle. Focus? Drive? Motivation? You better believe it. I will never go back to where I was. That pain... that guilt... those feelings of insignificance. Never.

Greater than any of these, however, is forgiveness. I have learned how to be kinder to myself. I have discovered that I will never be capable of accepting love or loving someone else if I do not first love myself. A cliché? Perhaps. But a deep truth, nonetheless. One that escaped me for far too many years. Being my own best friend has been the most eye-opening experience of my life. It has allowed confidence to replace arrogance, wellness to overcome self-destruction, and social empowerment to remove isolation.

I am having friends over to my apartment for the UFC fights tonight. I am excited to once again feel good about organizing social events and allowing people into my private space. As I get out of the shower and get ready for the evening, I look again into the mirror. A different person looks back. Not perfect, but more capable of being happy than at any other time in my life. Let's get ready to rumble!

Pater Familias:

Saulo Ribeiro is larger than life. For months I have heard my coaches and teammates speak of the man in respectful tones as they relate tales of his world championships and his renowned ability to communicate jiu jitsu to others. He is the head of the Ribeiro Jiu Jitsu association, and he is standing right in front of me. I am, quite simply, in awe.

When I found out that Saulo was coming to do a seminar for us, I watched videos of his matches. He is more than just a champion – he has beaten some of the biggest names in the sport. He is also the founder of the University of Jiu Jitsu, which is an innovative approach to teaching jiu jitsu and the basis for the handbook that Five Rings uses as an academy. The opportunity to learn some great things has presented itself and I want to make the most of it. He came to observe Five Rings members and offer feedback on our training last night and now he is conducting an open seminar.

This isn't the first time I have been around celebrities; I attended Yale University and there were more than a few big name stars that went to school with me there (Jennifer Connolly, Sara Gilbert, Christie Martin, heck... Josh Saviano was in my fraternity and played Paul Pfeiffer on the Wonder Years). This is different, though. I am aware of what it takes for this man to have accomplished the things that he has: the hard work, the dedication, the years of training and perseverance, as well as the passion to bring his style and message to those who would learn from him. I feel honored to be in his presence.

I feel some surprise when I see how friendly and warm Saulo is as he walks among my Five Rings brothers and sisters. There is a great turnout for the seminar and he makes a point of trying to greet all of us personally with a smile and offer some words of encouragement. His Brazilian background is evidenced by a strong accent that I find oddly endearing. One thing strikes me quite profoundly. If I am not mistaken, he is approximately the same age that I am. Wow.

He gathers us for warm-ups and it quickly becomes apparent that we are in for something different than we are used to. The exercises are a bit more traditional to the point of being a little formal. I am impressed by how intense some of the activities are and at how the movements loosen up some different muscles than I am used to. Saulo is akin to a cheerleader, in that he keeps us pumped up and excited all the time. I don't think I've ever smiled quite this much while doing calisthenics.

Coach Tom says of Saulo, and I quote – "He is a master of teaching techniques in a simple, easy to understand way that is immediately applicable and usable in one's game." I notice this for myself almost from the start of the seminar. I am severely lacking in my bottom guard game. The attacks that I feel comfortable with from that position are basically non-existent. This is not from lack of instruction, either. I just haven't found that base from which I feel comfortable moving and creating space. It may stem to some degree from that fact that being on my back or even on an edge is still kind of foreign to me. As a wrestler, exposing your back to the mat was about as 'wrong' as something could be. That being said, Saulo just demonstrated a position that he calls 'classic guard'. From closed guard you break down your opponent's posture using a cross lapel grip and a same side sleeve grip (hand position #3!). As they attempt to recover, you open your guard and place your sleeve grip side heel in their hip and the other heel into their shoulder, bicep, or other hip. Your grips give you pull, while your heel placement gives you the opportunity to extend their body. If done properly, you gain a lot of control over your opponent and Saulo demonstrates several different attacks from that base position (arm bar, triangle, cross choke, omaplata, and sweep). I feel my pulse quicken as I start to understand the possibilities. A few drills later I become even more excited at the level of comfort I feel from this position. I think I may have just found my guard bottom 'go-to' starting point.

I am extremely grateful to have the opportunity to learn from a six time world champion. His accomplishments are not something that I personally aspire to at this point in my life, but the way he carries himself and interacts with others are definitely traits that I would like to acquire. His method of teaching is effective and seemed to offer something to everyone in the room. I wonder if I could ever coach jiu jitsu. That would be an amazing way for me to get back into teaching. Food for thought, for sure.

An unusual urge comes over me as the seminar comes to a close... I find myself wanting this man's autograph! I don't think I've ever felt this way before. What the heck, I may as well run with it. I've experienced a lot of new things lately so it just feels right to go with this one. Everybody needs a hero to look up to.

Addiction:

Is this the sixth, seventh, or eighth class I've been to this week? I lose track sometimes. I find myself coming to Five Rings more and more often. I go to morning and evening classes pretty much every day and they recently started up a midday class that fits my schedule on Mondays and Wednesdays as well.

The instructor, Greg, is a purple belt that recently started training with us after moving here from California. Great guy, even if he is a Patriots fan. Seriously, how anyone still likes that team after my G-men crushed their 'perfect' season back in '07 escapes me. Anyhow, his perspective and coaching style are very different from Coach Tom's and Coach Eric's. I find myself feeling more and more well-rounded after each of his sessions, particularly when he teaches a move I already think I know from an angle that I didn't consider before.

We've got another tournament on the horizon. This one is called the Grappling X. It's an independently run competition and we're taking a small crew of people out to compete. Still, I'm pretty excited to get back on the mat. So, I guess that could be one reason that I'm up here so much. But if I'm being completely honest with myself then I have to acknowledge the other reasons, too. I'm getting addicted to the social network I have established, as well as the positive growth and changes in my body and fitness level. It's nice to feel like I'm learning something every time I come here, too. It wasn't that long ago that my addictions were a lot less healthy and a lot more detrimental to my well-being.

I remember the first time I stepped into the casino and sat down at the tables. Yeah, on top of being a smoker and an alcoholic, I was a gambling addict to boot. There was a difference, though. Nicotine and alcohol had their claws in me early in life and didn't represent much of anything but an ongoing disease that I never treated. Gambling was something new. A true psychological escape. That first time I started putting real money down I realized that I could lose myself in the rush. I didn't have to think about what my wife was doing behind my back while I commuted two hundred miles (anywhere from five to seven hours) from Palm Springs to Los Angeles and back every day. I didn't have to worry about the unpaid bills or the birthday present for my stepson that I couldn't afford or that sneaking suspicion that my co-workers at school knew something was wrong with me. All I had to worry about was that next card. The next roll of the dice. The lie that I could tell myself to make it all okay: "One big payday is all you need to turn things around, Dan. Just a little bit of luck."

I remember the calls from my wife that I would ignore because I didn't want to hear her yell. Even worse were the ones from my stepsons that I would ignore because I was too ashamed to tell them that I'd blown my entire paycheck again. I even hit the big payday more than once, only to walk out of the casino doors having lost it all. It was then that I knew that it wasn't about the money. It was about getting away from the misery my life had become in the easiest way I could find. Then came the borrowed money (family, coworkers, payday loans) followed not too long after by losing the house, losing the job, and almost losing my life. I'd become really, really good at losing. In retrospect, I realize that it's a pattern. I'd developed a habit; an addiction, if you will, to losing. It's like I was searching for the bottom of the barrel. And then, I finally found it.

It's difficult to relate my current experience of falling in love with the art of jiu jitsu as an addiction because of all the negative associations that I have with that word. I even went so far as to look it up to see if it really was fitting. The dictionary definition does mandate that there are negative consequences associated with an addiction, so since I am finding it very difficult to identify any that result from the time I spend at the gym I am going to modify my descriptor to a habit. I wonder if I can make up my own terminology and call it a 'positive addiction'. Why not?

I do feel like I am at the tables sometimes when I get to Five Rings. It is an escape, of sorts, but more like the way meditation is an escape. I feel like I am getting myself 'right' when I am working out or rolling with my friends. I most definitely am not avoiding anything. Nor do I feel any shame. Just the opposite! I feel proud and enlightened and ecstatic when I am here. If this is a new addiction, then I wouldn't have it any other way. My coaches are 'enabling' me to be a healthy, contributing member of society again. The friends I have made definitely make me 'high' with the laughter and love that I feel when we hang out.

As summer rolls on, my jiu jitsu game continues to improve. It's a heck of a lot better than my poker game ever was.

Dedication:

There are three things that I promised myself when I walked away from the car crash last Halloween. Three things that I knew had to change or I was going to become a statistic. Or worse. Some of these things were ideas that had been floating around in my head for months, but that for one reason or another I couldn't commit to doing. Almost killing yourself and someone else has a way of motivating change.

The first promise I made was to never take another drink or put anything into my body that would cause me to lose my decision making ability. Never again would the excuse – "But I was drunk" come out of my mouth. No more apologies for saying or doing something that I only vaguely remember in the first place. Drugs and alcohol would no longer play a role in my life or be the demon that led me astray.

Perhaps this might come as a surprise to some, but this has been the easiest promise for me to keep. It has been as 'easy' as not putting a glass or bottle to my lips. The images of flashing lights and screams that bubble up in my head every time I think about drinking discourage the activity to a great degree. And every day that I don't take a drink helps to reinforce not taking one as well. The smiles from new friends; never having to deal with a hangover; being able to get on the mat and roll every day! These things are supremely motivating.

The second promise was to stop taking my life for granted. I am not a religious person, nor do I imagine that I will ever be. But as I realized how close to death I came (again) it became apparent that there are some things in this world that I can and cannot control. If I did not take command of the things that I could actively participate in then I was simply floating on the breeze – allowing the world to push me where it would and fall when it chose. I promised to give myself wings. Not enough to stop the rare strike of lightning, but something to let me dictate where I would go and what I would do.

Jiu jitsu is the framework of the wings of my life. Like Daedalus, I have worked hard to construct a lasting mechanism to be able to fly straight and escape from the bondage of my past. The routine of training and the discipline of the 'gentle' art give me the foundation to build a better future on. The relationships and support network that I have established are the feathers for those wings. Amazing friendships and stronger family ties have given me the ability and confidence to take risks and go places that I never thought I would see again… or ever, in some cases. But to avoid the pain of his eventual loss (his son, Icarus, flew too close to the sun) I have come to realize that the wax holding the feathers is my resolve. My decisions will ultimately determine where and when I will land or if I will crash before finding that resting place.

It is a little more difficult to explain the third promise. There was a time in my life when I felt like a leader of people. An example that others could look up to. Back in high school I was the captain of three varsity sports teams and the valedictorian of my class. It was a great feeling to know that others looked to me for guidance or wisdom, even if it at that point the parameters of my knowledge were much narrower than they are now. My third promise was a vow to rediscover that leader in me; to become someone who was able to share the successes and failures of his life with the hopes that others could find inspiration or take comfort in them. This promise has been the hardest to keep. It has been a challenge to reach beyond myself and consider the needs of others, but I slowly find opportunities arising to do so. Whether it is the new white belt asking for help with a move or a friend that just needs someone to listen to them or my niece and nephew needing help with their math homework there are now times when I am able to give of myself and feel like what I am giving is not tainted by the selfishness and pain of the past.

Promises are funny things. They are only as strong as the person that makes them. I am becoming stronger every day. And as time passes these three promises are leading me to a treasure I thought was long lost to me - integrity.

Relation:

There are times when I am rolling that it occurs to me that the harder I strain to make a position or move happen, the easier it becomes for my partner to escape or gain the upper hand. On the other hand, sometimes when I bide my time and wait for an opening then I can secure control and get a dominant position. I've made active strides towards phasing out the 'Grrr'- jitsu aspects of my game by focusing on being technical, patient, and relaxed.

A few months ago I started dating again. It was a difficult decision to put myself back into the scene. By putting time into my recovery and into achieving my personal goals, I have felt the greatest improvements in the most meaningful areas of my life. To be quite honest, I was most motivated by loneliness. It has been years and years since I lived completely on my own and longer than that since I was single for any length of time. So I decided to give online dating a try. As I've learned recently, sometimes taking a risk can reap great rewards.

The woman I met was, in short, a wonderful person. We communicated well and had fun when we spent time together. Over a few months and several dates we got to know about each other – backgrounds, interests, goals. I felt like I was going about the relationship building in the 'right' way, if there is such a thing. I had a great deal of respect for her and appreciated her candor when it came to how she felt about me. She felt like we might have a good future together if I was willing to commit more of myself to the relationship.

I had decided to try to get to know my partner without rushing into the physical aspect of the relationship. Initially, this was motivated by wanting to take things slowly in order to see if everything else worked between us. As time went on, I realized that, at least for my part, the 'spark' was missing. It occurs to me that many of my friends have expressed this kind of sentiment when dating, but it was a new experience for me. Generally, if some part of the equation was good in the past I would try to force the rest of the issue. Make things work, as it were. Every single one of those relationships progressed with a good share of drama and ended badly, for one person or the other or both.

My new friend is now telling me with tears in her eyes that she doesn't want to continue dating me. I have been honest with her about my feelings all the way through our dating process and she has realized that she wants more than I have to offer. I am deeply saddened by her choice, but I can feel nothing but respect for her. She is choosing to move on rather than to try to change me to fit her needs. I realize as she walks out the door that I am proud of myself for standing my ground and not giving into an easier emotional course of action. I will be ready when I'm ready. I will know that person who I want to share my life with when I find them and I won't feel the need to force anything.

For now, I will continue to work on me. I still have these gaping holes in my emotional, mental, and physical selves. I am making progress and I feel great about how far I've come. But it is patience and fortitude that will get me to my ultimate goals – feeling comfortable in my own skin, having the confidence to take on anything life throws at me, and sharing of myself in healthy ways. My loneliness is an extension of insecurities that I am trying to leave behind. It isn't easy. I am starting to believe that most, if not all, things in life that are worth pursuing require some obstacles to be overcome and challenges to be met.

This is a major turning point for me, however, and I must recognize it as such. The past had shown me to be incapable of the kind of maturity I feel like I demonstrated in dealing with this relationship. Not only did I stay true to myself, but the honesty and patience with which I handled things prevented both of us from greater pain in the future. Pain that I used to pursue with the same passion that I now chase health and growth. Life lessons rarely stand out so clearly and I feel grateful that I can acknowledge this one as much as I can.

Patience. Focus. Determination. I'm getting there.

Resurrection:

The summer breeze on this fine mid-June day blows over my freshly buzzed scalp as I walk up the hill to Five Rings. I revel in the warmth of the sun and in the chance to once again get on the mat and improve my game. This is definitely a high point in my life.

It's been over three years since I hit the lowest point in my life. My memories of it are still as vivid as if it happened yesterday, when I let myself think about it:

I can hear the seagulls cry in the distance. The salt spray from the ocean coats my lips and fills my nostrils. The bright sunshine tries to pierce through my closed eyelids. I feel the sand give way beneath my fingers and toes as my muscles begin to relax. This is the first time in years that I can filter each sense so distinctly. I definitely could have chosen a worse place to die. I've always loved the beach.

I found out last night that my wife cheated on me. With a 'friend' who also just happened to be her meth dealer. She's been lying to me for years about the drugs. The infidelity was more recent. Or who knows… maybe she's been sleeping around during our whole marriage. It doesn't matter anymore, really. All I can seem to do is think about what a chump I've been. I really should have known better. So many red flags along the way, from the very beginning 'til now.

When we met there was so much passion, so much infatuation – I'd never felt that way before. And she needed me so badly. So I gave her everything. My whole life. I took care of her two children, her niece, and her father. Defended her when everyone else abandoned her. All I ever wanted in return was her respect and her love. What I got slowly ate away at my heart, and then finally drove a stake through it.

I went into the casino this morning instead of going to work. It was my last ditch effort, my request to the universe to show me a sign that

I still had some unfinished business here in this existence. If I won, I'd start over. Find a new purpose. But I didn't win. I didn't want to; wouldn't have stopped playing until it was all gone anyhow. I saved enough for one last pack of cigarettes and a bottle of sleeping pills.

The fuzziness blurs the edges of my vision and consciousness starts to fade. Soon the pain will end. For me, at least. One last selfish act that will probably destroy everything that I tried to build. But I don't care. I just want the misery to go away. The crashing of the waves carries me into the unknown.

Darkness overcomes me.

Frantic pounding confuses me. No more sunlight burning. Waves still crashing, but the sirens and voices force them into the background. Someone shoves a tube down my throat and the pain comes crashing back. I'm not dead. After all the failures, you'd think I'd at least get this one right. I curse the paramedic as I recognize him for what he is. I reach out to hug him when I realize what I had almost done.

Over the next few weeks, family and friends that I thought I'd closed out forever return and with the help of therapists convince me that there are still things worth living for. I am still miserable, but I keep waking up each day because I don't want them to be sad. The medication flattens me out. Time goes by... slowly.

It wasn't until months later that my brother, Dylan, came to get me away from the hell fires of Southern California. The rains of Oregon slowly started to wash away the past. But my subconscious self still writhed in emotional turmoil. I had no direction. The distance between us did not stop me from thinking about my wife or my sons or the life I had left behind. It would take years for me to 'move on'.

The memory of the end of that part of my life doesn't grieve me like it once did. I celebrate that day as a moment of enlightenment. I would not value the amazing things that I have since discovered if I had not been in that dismal predicament. The beauty and kindness that I experience on a daily basis from those that truly care about me shine that much brighter because of that day. The infirmity of my hospitalization make me value my health and ability to roll with my new friends that much more.

I am glad I didn't die that day. I am committed to one day making a difference in the lives of those that may believe as I once did... that they don't have anything left to give. For now, I am content to walk up this road and into the gym and focus on becoming someone that I like to be around. Soon enough, I will have the reserves and confidence to share my story with the world.

Actualization:

I feel like I am hitting my stride. I recently earned my second stripe and my 'A' game is starting to develop. My 'classic' guard drilling has allowed me to feel more and more comfortable being aggressive and attacking for submissions. I'm still not always able to finish them, but I definitely feel like I have viable options from that position. The Grappling X tournament is quickly approaching and my confidence level is at an all-time high.

As the days of summer meander by, I get the sense that everything is coming together. My addictions no longer control my life. The insecurities that had such influence over my choices have fallen by the wayside. Progress and accomplishment have replaced stagnation and failure. Physically and mentally I feel stronger than ever. Emotionally, I still struggle at times but only when I dwell overlong on my past. When I focus on the present, life is good.

I liken the recent course of my life journey to that of a lesson learned from Coach Nick recently at a 'Church of Jiu Jitsu' session. Part of my struggles to finish submissions from my chosen guard position has been my inability to relax at key moments and let my opponent close space. Nick had me drill and free roll while consciously focusing on my breathing and relaxation. This allowed the triangles and arm bars to become tighter and more controlled. The challenges that I face on a daily basis also seem easier to deal with when I allow myself to relax, think, and reason out how to handle them.

Jiu jitsu is providing an excellent foundation for me to build a life of fulfillment and purpose. I've long been a proponent of an existential outlook. There are a ton of examples in everyday society that show that if you believe in something strongly enough, your belief can influence reality. For a long time, I lost sight of that philosophy and allowed the currents of other's choices (and often my own poor ones) to drag me along. I relish the feelings of achievement when I look in the mirror or successfully perform a new move during rounds. These are sensations that have long been missing in my life.

There can be no doubt that there are still holes to be filled in. Financially, I've limited my ability to choose. I made a conscious decision months ago to simplify my avenues of income in an effort to reduce stress and allow myself time in my schedule to pursue personal growth. I can foresee a time in the not-so-distant future where this may need to change. To be blunt, I can't keep living on $400 a month and hope that there won't be any budget emergencies. Maybe I can start working on my novel again soon. Or some other writing project that might kick start my dream of turning that into a source of income.

I also realize that it would be nice to have someone to share my ups and downs with. The friends that I am making are truly amazing and I wouldn't trade them for anything. But I think it would be pretty swell to add a 'someone special' to my life. I'm not going to settle for just anyone this time around though. It is going to be someone spectacular; someone with the same passion and drive that I have discovered in myself. I don't feel the need to rush this one, though. I am content to continue working on me. I'd be lying if I said I hadn't noticed a particular someone lately though. She keeps finding her way into my thoughts.

Self-actualization is defined as the achievement of one's full potential through creativity, independence, spontaneity, and a grasp of the real world. If you had asked me seven months ago if I thought that this was a realistic goal then I probably would have chuckled and sighed and mumbled something about pipe dreams. This is no longer the case. I believe, once more, that I can reach that potential.

Camaraderie:

The Grappling X tournament is being held at a college gymnasium out in an eastern suburb of Portland. It is small and has only three mats, but as we arrive I anticipate a fun and compelling day of competition. I have trained hard and worked to develop an applicable set of skills that should serve me well.

I check the bracket and discover that I am not only the first match of the day, but that I also only have one opponent. Such is the way of things for those of us that compete in the Master's divisions of local tournaments. Since we are guaranteed at least two matches, we'll have to win the best two of three contests for the gold medal.

As I warm-up, I notice the other 'older' competitors hanging around as they wait for their turn to get on the mat. We all introduce ourselves and chat about our experiences with jiu jitsu at our various gyms and our expectations for the day. I even meet my opponent, David. He is very tall! We all offer wishes for a good tournament and get ready to start our matches. This seems to be a universal trait of jiu jitsu tournaments. I can't corroborate it for the younger athletes, but there is a true spirit of sportsmanship and respect for those of us who have been around the block.

Five Rings has brought a solid crew of fifteen teammates today and I feel their strong support as I step onto the mat. The cheers boost my confidence and I attack immediately, going straight for the classic guard position that I've been training. I slide into guard poorly, grips loose and barely maintaining contact with my heel. My opponent's length is making things difficult, but I persist. I disengage briefly and then renew my offense. This time my grips are tight and I slowly work my legs into an arm bar/triangle pit stop. As I step over to finish the arm bar, David taps and I have won. All in all, it has taken about thirty-five seconds.

Coach Eric congratulates me on my victory and prepares me for the next matchup. I notice that Coach Greg and Coach Nick are also in my corner. These three have been integral to my progress thus far, and it is heartening to see them all there. My teammates shout their support from the stands. I get the chance to watch a new friend from Seaside BJJ compete before I have to tackle David one more time.

As we begin, it is obvious that his coach has given him good advice. He quickly pulls guard on me, almost knocking me off balance in the process. I work to pass his guard, using a shin slide technique I learned recently. I get to half guard and then push the other leg through to cross sides position. But wait, I'm not getting the points. I hear Eric yelling for me to get my arm free of his legs. I stack him up in order to do so, but he flips us both over. Finding a burst of speed, I explode off my back into quarters position. I just went from a dominant position to a much less desirable one so I try to breathe and relax. I use an old wrestling technique called the duck out and almost get to his back. We end up back in quarters and when I try to duck out again, he rotates his legs over and locks in a guillotine choke.

I feel fine for a moment, comfortable that I am on top and in control. Then I mistakenly step into his guard. Darkness enters my peripheral vision and I struggle to create space and keep blood flowing to my head. I listen for my coach's voice. "Step away, pop your head out... posture up!" I try to follow the instructions, but it is a close call before I can finally escape. The fact that I am gurgling encourages my opponent and he squeezes for all he's worth. After what seems an eternity, his arms loosen and I seize the opportunity to lift my head. I can tell that David is exhausted, so I drive through to mount and ride out the match comfortably ahead on points. Another victory and the gold medal are mine!

I cheer on the rest of my teammates: Noah, Evan, Ziggy, Natan, Liz, Preston, Matt, Robert, and the rest all give their all. At the end of the day we've taken home eleven medals and some fantastic experience.

More than my victory, I value the sense that I am now a part of a team. Jiu jitsu is an individual sport and when you step on the mat it is you against the person standing across the mat. But your team and coaches are the ones that make sure you are ready to be there. I felt like every one of my training partners was standing there on the mat with me today and my victory is as much theirs as it is mine.

Examination:

Coach Tom is talking to us about having an appropriate mindset when we step on the mat. He says we need to understand the difference between 'gym jitsu' and 'tournament jiu jitsu'. I think I get the message. Basically, when we are training our goal should be to improve our skills and to help our training partners improve as well. Competition changes that goal to imposing our will and showcasing the skills that we've learned. This lesson goes hand in hand with some other ideas that Tom has shared with us – 'intensity with a smile' and 'elegant ass-kicking' are his personal extensions of the fundamental tenet of *arte suave,* "the gentle art". Jiu jitsu is the art of timing and of coordination. It is so much more than technique and flexibility. There is a mindset that comes with progress in the sport. A confidence that comes from understanding what your body is capable of.

I recognize very clearly that I have not progressed to a level where I can draw upon a wellspring of certainty. I still struggle with demons of the past, both those that I am aware of and those that still hide themselves in my subconscious. What I have been able to accomplish, however, is to rebuild a foundation of health from which to face those challenges. Replacing unhealthy habits with productive ones, eliminating stressors by simplification, focusing on the positive possibilities of a new day; these have been the keys to my success.

So the connection that becomes apparent to me is that I'm establishing a solid 'gym jitsu' game in my life. As long as I am able to maintain control of my environment, whether by surrounding myself with a solid support network of caring friends and family or staying solidly in my comfort zone, I am able to feel like I am moving forward towards a sense of completion and wholeness. The more difficult test lies ahead. It is time to start taking risks. I miss the highs and lows that come with putting my whole heart and self into my life endeavors. Just like training in the gym though, I need to prepare myself for the unexpected. I can think of several things that should help.

As far as my addictions are concerned, there are going to be quite a few opportunities to test myself in the near future. I'm headed back East to my 20th high school reunion soon and I'm going to be around folks I used to party with. I fervently believe that I'm strong enough to handle it. Cigarettes, alcohol, and gambling have no place in my life anymore.

I am also starting a blog that I can share with anyone who cares to read it. It's for me, but if others get some use of it then the benefit becomes all the greater. I find that when I write things down it grounds me and the life lessons that I hope to share. The strongest impetus I feel to put my words into text is to reconcile the time from my DUI to present day with the life that happened before it. I think there is power and fortitude to be found in that connection. I feel so differently now than I did then. Some days it seems like I am an entirely new person.

I've also registered for American Nationals. It's in Los Angeles at the end of September. This will be a major test for my jiu jitsu progress, but an even bigger one for my mental and emotional health. L.A. is where my life got turned upside down and almost ended. My stepsons are still there and I am making plans to see them. I believe that I am ready to face whatever may come. I am no longer afraid. The tournament of life has a new competitor as well.

Uncertainty:

Tuesday night tournament rounds at the gym can be enlightening, educational, and inspiring. Tonight they are downright depressing! I try to implement my 'A' game as I prepare for Nationals and it just isn't working. I'm getting my guard passed over and over again. I search for positives to cling to, but there don't seem to be many. This is getting rougher by the moment. It is extremely frustrating and more than a bit disheartening. I have been drilling and working this technique for a while now. I should have some success with it 'in the wild' by this point.

Let's call a spade a spade, shall we? Insecurity is a demon we all face at some point or another. My lack of confidence has been a perpetual monkey on my back for years. I used to put on a good show, but anyone that took the time to get to know me could see past it very quickly. This uncertainty often got the better of me – I would lie and cheat, take the easy way out, avoid the problem. I escaped through online fantasy games so that I wouldn't have to face reality. That addiction translated into the gambling issue later in life. I am certain it played a role in my alcoholism as well.

I still struggle from time to time. Not nearly as much as in the past, but patterns of behavior and habits of dealing with people and the world can be difficult to change without appropriate motivation. I feel like I have a lot of positive motivators these days: my competitive drive, the prospect of new learning, reinforcement from friends. I need to be more forgiving of myself when I slip and fall. I am definitely my own worst critic at times. At other times, the people who might have been the most understanding made different choices that influenced my current insecurity.

I will never forget the look in her eyes when I told her we wouldn't have enough money to get everything on the boys' Christmas lists. Disappointment intermingled with disgust. I told her I'd make it up

to them. We'd go someplace special after my next paycheck. "You're such a chump, Dan – I don't know why I married you. You can't take care of us. You can't do anything right." I dodge the ashtray she throws at me and it shatters the sliding glass door behind me. More bills to pay. She's right, too. If I weren't a chump, I would have left years ago. I wouldn't put up with all this bullshit. Or would I? Maybe this is the best I can ask for. My boys are so strong. I can be strong for them, too.

My new sense of integrity drives me to tell Coach Eric about my struggles during rounds. If I repress this frustration, it is going to come out in some ugly ways. He looks me in the eye and says, 'Dude, I have felt what you are feeling a hundred times or more. It comes with the territory, my friend. This isn't tiddlywinks here, its jiu jitsu. When you 'lose', you learn. You are getting better whether you can see it right now or not. Keep training. Mat time is the key.'

Really? Is it that easy? He hasn't steered me wrong yet, so I make a conscious effort to re-evaluate my experience and perspective. Alright, so my best moves were getting beaten on a regular basis tonight. I've been doing this for about 8 months now. The majority of the people I roll with have multiple years of experience. Could I recognize what they were doing and modify my positioning to make my game plan more effective? Absolutely. Okay. This feels better; mentally, if not emotionally. I resolve to persevere. Nationals are only a couple of weeks away.

Reunion:

It's been twenty years since I graduated from high school. Twenty years. I find it interesting to note that the last time I approached life with the same fervor and enthusiasm as I do now is probably around the time of that graduation. I was valedictorian of my class, captain of three varsity sports, and headed to an Ivy League university – the classic overachiever. I firmly believed that the world was a place that was waiting to be conquered. Hard work and natural born talent were going to be enough to accomplish any goal that I set.

I had a rude awakening waiting for me out in the 'real world'. I was ill prepared for the challenges that I had to face: the lures of alcohol and addiction hooked me hard once I left the safe confines of my small, sheltered town in upstate New York. Still, it is with a joyful heart that I return to that town and the school where I grew up. I am excited to see family and friends and reconnect with people that I haven't seen since high school.

I fly out of Seattle and into Boston because it is significantly cheaper than a flight directly from Portland to Albany. I also have friends that I want to visit in each of those cities. Jonas is heading to the Navy soon and it is good to see him, even if it is only for a short while. We play some pool and talk about the changes in our lives. He is doing everything he can to be a good father and husband, but it obviously isn't easy. Eli seems to be thriving on the opposite coast, and he reminds me that despite the progress I've made I need to keep the future in mind.

I also get the chance to visit with a high school sweetheart in Boston. Terri is a Harvard grad who currently works as a surgeon. Seeing her gives me the opportunity to talk about my reservations about taking risks – she encourages me to pursue happiness, in whatever form I may find it. I resolve then and there to ask out the woman who caught my eye at the gym as soon as I return from this trip. Life is way too short to miss out on someone like her.

It turns out that a friend of a friend is heading to my next stop from Boston, so I finagle a ride and end up outside of Saratoga. Temptation waits for me there in the form of an old drinking buddy (Shaggy) and is balanced by the presence of my oldest childhood friend, Sean. Shaggy Bob's life reflects the roller coaster ride that mine has been, but he has recently found the Yin to his Yang... a great girl named Erin who appreciates him for who he is... flaws and all. I break down and try to smoke a cigarette for old time's sake and nearly throw up after one drag. That is one habit I won't be picking back up anytime soon. The more dangerous temptation of alcohol is easier to resist. Sean's presence is supportive and Bob does his best to not push the issue. We have a blast reminiscing, playing darts, and getting reacquainted after all the years that have gone by. Even in the face of Shaggy's annual Manifest Boozery Landmine Croquet, I am able to stay completely sober and reinforce that wisdom that I can have fun without alcohol.

I am very excited and nervous for tomorrow. I get to see what has changed and what has not. Opportunities for growth shall most certainly present themselves, if only I can take advantage of them.

Reunion: (cont.)

Sean and I pass by familiar places. I laugh as I realize that even after all this time, so much looks and feels the same. There are changes, for sure, but one of the reasons I love where I grew up is that there is continuity... stability. I could drive most of these roads blindfolded. Spending time with Sean is amazing. He listens as I describe the details of my journey over the past year, asking probing questions and adding sage anecdotes at appropriate times. I have always admired him. Just like my hometown, he is a rock that I count on. Not unchanging, but steady. One of my heroes in life, even if I've never come right out and told him so. I think he knows anyhow.

We've been searching for places to roll. Small towns aren't necessarily known for their abundance of mat space, particularly on the weekend. We strike out, but the BJJ conversation is intense! Sean collects martial arts info like some people collect stamps. I always learn something new when we talk. I promise him that sooner than later we will have a chance to test our jits skills. It is hard to describe how ecstatic I feel to be able to make that promise. It wasn't that long ago that I could barely walk up a flight of stairs without getting winded.

The reunion isn't for a few hours, so I go to visit with Sean's family and my family. My nieces have grown so much; reminding me that time passes inexorably so we must make the most of it while we can. We stop to visit my mother, alone with her cats tucked away in the Adirondack foothills home where my brothers and I were raised. Not by her, but by my grandparents. Our mother left when I was three and came back when I was sixteen. She is a survivor, even if she is struggling a bit at the moment. She is always excited when I visit, which isn't nearly as much as I would wish.

I take a few minutes at Sean's house to clean up and get my 'good' clothes on. I dress up so rarely these days. I think I only own one tie and that spends most of its time hanging in the closet. I realize as I am getting ready that I'm not as nervous as I thought I might be. The people I went to high school with will have grown and changed, suffered and triumphed just as I have. If nothing else, their capacity for understanding should have improved.

I walk into the restaurant where our event is being held and spot some familiar faces almost immediately. Lori and Heidi worked diligently to organize the reunion and I thank them for the opportunity to come together and reminisce. Stacey, Nicole, and Lou were my neighbors in the tiny 'suburb' of Hampton. I find it to be an interesting societal commentary that even in the confines of rural upstate New York proximity can still dictate the closeness of relationships to a certain degree. It is exciting to see old friends and acquaintances, to talk of our lives and how things have changed and how other things have stayed the same. I am very proud to be healthy and happy at this moment in my life. I touch base with Jason, another recovering alcoholic. He's been sober for five years and gives me wise advice about how to keep on keeping on. "It never stops being one day at a time, Dan. Just keep waking up and keeping your perspective."

I spot two of the people I dreaded seeing. Paula and I had butted heads on more than one occasion in high school, mostly because I was an arrogant prick. Megan had a penchant for talking about me behind my back and some of the things that made their way through the grapevine bordered on cruel. I had already figured out how I was going to handle these encounters on the plane ride here, so I take a deep breath and approach Paula first. I outline what I felt to be my transgressions and apologize on behalf of my younger self. She laughs and says that she does remember, but that it wasn't that big of a deal to her. Life has moved on and she understands that we were kids. Kids can be mean, ya know? Megan has already had a few drinks. She actually asks me to dance. She has changed a lot since high school. I decide not to confront her about things that honestly don't bother me that much anymore, taking a page from Paula's book of forgiveness.

As the evening winds down, I am struck by the surreal nature of this scene. Twenty years have passed and as I look around the room I see so much that has changed, but even more that has remained constant. The cliques are still there, if a little less obvious. Best friends in high school are still best friends now in some cases. Our one significant commonality (the fact that we all went to high school together) is enough to allow for the differences that might normally separate us. This is a lot more comfortable and enjoyable then what I expected.

I leave the reunion and spend the rest of the evening with Sean's family. Amazing people – they are a source of constant comfort and enlightenment for me. I feel very lucky to know them. It was only a year ago when I came to visit last, but so much has changed. I was miserable then and they counseled me as best as they could, helping me to see some light on what seemed to be a fairly dismal horizon. Now I share the light of hope and passion and enthusiasm that I have found through jiu jitsu and friendship and wellness in the intervening months. This is a huge milestone for me and I know that I will never forget it.

Warrior:

Sitting across the table from one of the most electrifying people I've ever met highlights how far I've come in my journey to recovery – I feel confident and composed, even though the butterflies are ramming full speed against my stomach. Damn, she's gorgeous. She accepted my invitation to have dinner together – "for funzies". Still not sure whether she understands that I am completely enamored of her, but we're having a great time so I try not to worry about it too much. It's important to me that she sees me for who I am. In the past I often put up a façade in order to seem more appealing, guessing at what I thought the other person wanted and completely missing the mark. This time would be different. I like who I am now, and if she doesn't then I am finally in a place where I'm okay with that. Life will go on.

By the end of the evening, after some scintillating conversation, great food, and a romantic walk, my hopes are high. I see something in her that radiates positivity. She's bright and passionate and seems to have similar goals to mine. I can absolutely feel chemistry between us. The spark is most assuredly there. We part ways with huge smiles on our faces. I can't wait to see her again!

A while back, Robert, Liz, and I registered to compete in the Warrior Dash. It's a five kilometer obstacle course meant to test your speed and willpower. It routinely draws around eight thousand competitors over two days. I am very excited to compete, as I haven't done any racing since my early college days. I'm in decent shape as I have been hitting the roads as often as possible so I think I should do fairly well. I am also excited to spend more time with Liz and to see if she's as dominant on a race course as she is on a mat. Robert maintains that he doesn't run for training, but he's in great shape so I imagine he'll do well anyhow.

We meet at Five Rings. Liz made us patriotic outfits so we would look like a team and to honor the ten year anniversary of 9/11. The shredding makes us look badass and we add more decorations with markers and temporary tattoos. We drive out to the rural location where the race is being held and as we pull in we notice the traffic starting to build – there are a ton of people coming to this event! We can see an early heat of the race traversing an obstacle as we make our way to a parking spot. Our adrenaline is already starting to flow as we begin our search for the check-in.

Finding some other friends and acquaintances that we planned to meet proves to be less difficult than I first imagined, considering the crowds of people milling around the wooded area. I come face to face with one of the true tests of the day – besides being an intense race through the woods, the Warrior Dash is also a big party. Beer flows liberally and I can tell that some of the participants are more concerned with their buzz than with how well they do in the race. This is definitely the type of atmosphere where I would normally be pounding brews, but I honestly don't find it that hard to turn away from them. It isn't why I came and I won't let it distract me from achieving my goals for the day.

We form up at the starting line, casually bantering with the other competitors as we stretch out. A realization hits me hard as the time to begin rapidly approaches. I smoked cigarettes for almost twenty years, and here I am – about to run as fast as I can up steep hills and across daunting obstacles. How amazing is that? I've really done it. I'm reaching goals that I once thought were impossible. BANG! The starter's gun goes off and so do I. I sprint out of the gates and try to separate myself from the pack. The dust makes breathing and even seeing difficult at times, but the downslope allows a few of us who positioned ourselves well to get away from the main crush of racers. About a quarter of a mile into the race we hit our first inclines. These hills are steep and long, and do an excellent job of separating the folks who came to race and those who came for the party. As far as I can tell, I'm the first one of our team to hit the mile marker... and just as I think that, Liz blazes past me up the steepest part. Man, she is fast! At least for the moment, the trail becomes a lot more 'scenic'.

Several miles and a bunch of obstacles later, I finish the race. My lungs are burning – I definitely reached some of the damage caused by my years of smoking. My legs are dead. I am elated with my performance and would dance if I could move. I settle for a hug from Liz, who finished several minutes ahead of me and a high-five from Robert, who comes cruising in less than a minute behind me. We try to find our finishing times for a while, but the computers are being slow. We make our way slowly to the 'Car Wash' to clean up, taking pictures along the way. There is a moment where I put my arm around Liz and she leans her head into my shoulder. I know then that someday we'll be more than just friends, but for now all three of us revel in the moment. We celebrate being alive and the memories that we're making. I am finally learning to appreciate the present.

Life. Is. Good.

Nationals:

There haven't been too many times when I've missed not having my driver's license over the last nine months, but as I watch Robert settle into his ninth hour of driving on our way to Los Angeles for the IBJJF National Jiu-Jitsu Championship I really wish I could help out. I have to admit, though, that Robert is an absolute machine. He's showing no signs of fatigue even after all this time. We've stopped once to grab a bite to eat and refill the gas tank, but that's pretty much it.

It's been awesome getting to know Robert better. He comes from a small town, much like the one I grew up in... you know the one, where everyone knows everyone else and as he likes to put it, "The girls get pregnant just by you looking at them." He's undergone his own transformation over the last few years. He's lost a bunch of weight, quit drinking by his own choice, and dedicated a large portion of his life to jiu jitsu training and coaching. It's odd to think of someone almost 13 years my junior as a role model, but in truth he has been and continues to be that for me. He's dependable, dedicated, and a man of integrity. All things that I want to have associated with me.

We finally make it all the way through the drive and arrive in L.A. Memories start crashing through me. My life in Southern California was tumultuous, to say the least. Nine years of roller coaster craziness that left me clawing and scratching for breath. It is a significant moment to come back here, to see the familiar landmarks, to allow my mind to re-open those doors. My boys are waiting for me.

Our first stop, though, is also the first place I went to when I first arrived here in 1999. My Aunt Alta's house. She lives in Long Beach along with my Uncle Bob and they opened their home and their hearts to me when I was fresh out of grad school, giving me a solid foundation to get my feet underneath me in this new environment. It is really wonderful to see them both, in good spirits and good health, and Robert and I enjoy a good meal and great conversation.

We meet with Coach Tom and Coach Korbett (the head of the Ribeiro gym in Seattle) for dinner at an old roommate's restaurant. Fronk's has come a long way since Jamie opened it. The food is fantastic and the conversation ranges from game plans to the fact that Saulo himself will be competing in the tournament tomorrow. Thoroughly stuffed, Robert and I make our way to the hotel where Jerico awaits. Jerico is an interesting guy. A relatively new teammate, he's chosen to compete in the big tournaments early in his jiu jitsu career with mixed results. He's easy to get along with and we share some laughs.

Robert drops me off at my former in-laws house to meet with my sons. I haven't seen them in almost a year and a half. It is incredibly difficult to hold back the tears as they come out of the house, so I don't bother. They've gotten so big – and strong! Sammy is taller than I am now and lifts me off the ground when I hug him. Anthony, who was so small when I left, has hit his growth spurt and put on a bunch of muscle. We wrestle briefly and he is eager to demonstrate just how much muscle. They are so much the same, but so different, too! I can only imagine what they think of me. The last time they saw me I weighed 50 pounds more and reeked of cigarette smoke. I hope they are as proud of me as I am of them. Almost all of my ex-wife's family is there as well, and it quickly becomes apparent that at least in some small way I had an impact on all of these people's lives. Funny how I couldn't see that very clearly when I was living it. I resolve not to make that mistake with the people currently in my life. We wile away the hours reminiscing and sharing stories of what has transpired in the intervening months since we were last together. A couple of my ex-brother in-laws and my sons promise to come see me compete at the tournament and we hug and part ways again. I feel like my heart is being ripped out and it isn't long before I once again dissolve into tears.

I am finding it very hard to focus on the coming tournament. Luckily, I have a full day before I have to compete. My priorities seem very confused and I am struggling to understand why it has taken a jiu jitsu tournament for me to finally return to this place and the young men who are courageously trying to fill the gap that I left in their lives.

Nationals: - (cont.)

I do my very best to support my team. Five Rings and the Ribeiro association have become a family beyond my family. I get to see Coach Tom and Professor Saulo compete live for the first time and I am really excited to do so. I admire both of these men to a great degree and strive to pattern my new self after their example in many ways. It is an interesting role reversal to help my coach prepare for his matches. The atmosphere is different than at the local tournaments that I've been to so far; there is intensity in the air that is almost tangible. I sit with Robert and Jerico, surrounded by Ribeiro teammates from all along the West Coast.

The day meanders along, spiked by exciting high-profile matches; Caio Terra and Michael Liera Jr. put on a clinic in their divisions. The black belt divisions are supremely technical. I realize that I've become a bit of a jiu jitsu geek as I analyze each match. I watch as Coach Tom demonstrates a ton of technical skill and tenacity in his matches, only to fall to an opportunistic opponent who seems to have Coach's number at tournaments. Oddly, my esteem isn't diminished in the slightest. If anything, I find his grace and humility in defeat admirable and inspiring. I know for a fact that he's going to take this experience and use it as fuel for his next competition.

Saulo's matches draw a ton of attention, as one might expect for a world champion. He wins his divisions handily, demonstrating amazing technique and power along the way. I am awed to see jiu jitsu at this level first hand. There is simply no hesitation in the man. This is the result of an unshakable confidence in his ability to find a way to win. I vow to try to do the same in my matches.

(*...fast forward to the next day...*)

It's Sunday. Time for the whites and blues to show what they can do. Yep, that means me. I'm anxious, but confident that my coaches have prepared me well for success. All I can do at this point is give my best effort. My one concern is that due to my intense training (some folks might even say 'over' training) I've continued to lose weight. This means that even though when I registered for this event I was near the top of the middleweight class, I am now much closer to the bottom; I currently weigh 171 pounds. Ultimately, I remember that jiu jitsu is about technique and applied strength, not just how much you weigh. I hear my division being called so I go prepare myself for the coming battles.

My first match is against a guy named Troy from the Inland Empire. Yeah, I have to admit that I did some internet research on my opponents once they posted the brackets online. Not that it gave me any idea of who I am really up against, I found some comfort in making the effort if that makes any sense at all. As I step out onto the mat I look over to the stands where my sons and brothers-in-law sit. They made it! I am really excited to show them what I've learned.

My ears are ringing with Coach Tom's advice: "Impose your will, Dan. You know what you've trained. Be aggressive and get into your game." Okay. Let's see how this goes. We touch hands. I slide into classic guard smoothly. Pressure through the heel. Post other heel on the bicep. Adjust. Adjust. Feel his arm shift forward. Wham! I throw my leg over his face and lock in the arm bar. Tap. 35 seconds to achieve victory. Wow! That felt really, really good. Arm raised, big smile. Cheers and hugs. Time to get back to business. Next match is minutes away.

Steve is incredibly strong. He bulls me around the mat, tossing me like a rag doll. It is all I can do to stay on my feet! Fortunately for me, there isn't much purpose to his aggression. After the third time he drives me to my knees, I get smart. I use his momentum to slide into my favorite guard position and lock on the arm bar. He's having none of that, however. His strength again comes into play, along with poor positioning on my part. I can't finish the arm bar, but it doesn't stop me from trying. I grind his elbow into my groin, doing much more significant damage to myself than to him. He decides that a solid defense tactic to make me loosen the arm bar is to hoof me in the face. The ref misses it, but I don't let go. Minutes pass until it finally occurs to me to transition to a triangle choke. The shift in position distracts him long enough to allow me to pull his arm across to my opposite thigh and finish him with a differently leveraged arm bar. Same result as the first match: submission by arm bar. However, I have gassed myself hardcore. My forearms burn worse than I've ever experienced in my life and I can barely walk due to the damage I've caused my 'family jewels' by persisting in my original, poorly placed arm bar attempt.

The finals await. This is the National tournament and I've made the finals! One more opponent to go and I can bring home the gold medal to Five Rings. I look Coach Tom in the eye and ask him to tell me that I deserve this, that I've worked hard for it, and not to settle for silver. He does more than comply, pumping me up and reminding me to work my game. I stride to the center of the mat, ready to give it my best.

I had the luxury of watching Seton's matches. He won both of his previous matches by Ezekiel choke from mount. Unfortunately, he had the same luxury with me. He is painfully aware that sliding guard and attacking with an arm bar is my 'A' game. We touch hands, I slide guard and he lowers his center of gravity. This makes it incredibly hard to get to my pit stop and apply any submissions. It does, however, open him up to a sweep I've worked on. I use my cross collar grip to drive into him as I move my sleeve grip to his outside knee. He collapses onto his back as I come up into his half guard. Two points for me. I work to drive my leg across his locked in half guard and move to full mount, but in the process I allow him to under hook my nearside leg. He uses this leverage to escape, regain his feet, and start attacking my back. Desperately, I grab his ankle and drive into it. This forces him back to a north/south position. Here we remain for what seems like an eternity. I am locked underneath his weight, scooting him around the mat until we finally drive out of bounds. There is a little over a minute and a half left in the match. We meet again in the middle of that mat, touch hands, and I slide guard yet again. We fall out of bounds and the referee resets us once more. Forty seconds left. I'm still up by two points. I am completely and utterly exhausted. I try to throw my leg over for a triangle attempt, but Seton tilts his shoulders and passes my guard with relative ease. I struggle mightily to keep him at bay, but he is able to lock in a modified bow and arrow and I am done for. Twenty seconds is the difference between gold and silver on this day.

As I leave the mat, Coach gives me a look that indicates he believes that I could have and should have won the match, but it is quickly replaced by one of pride and he and my teammates give me high-fives. Some old friends, the Golds, have also come to watch. I used to tutor and babysit for them when I first moved to California. Jordan, Danny, and Zach have gotten so big! Jordan is a blue belt in his own right, but he didn't compete in this tournament. It is most excellent to see them.

Everything else falls to the periphery as I catch sight of my sons. The look in their eyes as they run up to congratulate me almost drives me to my knees. My breath catches in my throat as I see the pride radiating from them. They nearly crush me with their hugs and I am so happy that I am able to share this moment with them. Briefly, time stops… and we are a family again. I coached their Little League teams for years and encouraged them through their brief stints in wrestling clubs, but they never got a chance to see their Dad as a competitor. A healthy man who could set an example and be an athletic role model. Maybe it is too little, too late. But I wouldn't trade this moment for anything. Except maybe more of them.

Redemption:

Time is a funny thing. A moment can seem to last an eternity. A year can flash by in an instant. The last twelve months are a blur to me, but there are flashpoints that I can remember so vividly that it feels like they continue to happen inside my brain.

The recent calibration of belts at the gym means that in the larger world of jiu jitsu I am a white belt with four stripes. "On deck", as Coach Tom and Coach Eric like to call it. It means that the blues and purples will be 'testing' me over the next while to see if I'm ready to become a 'citizen'. I like that terminology and the message it carries. White belts are like supplicants; they are applying to earn the knowledge that will allow them to survive and thrive in the jiu jitsu community. Once the basic knowledge has been learned, the performance level shown, and the mat time committed then we become worthy of 'citizenship'.

I remember a time when the mysticism of martial arts was a turnoff for me. Now I understand more clearly that there has to be a certain amount of leeway for coaches to decide when someone is ready to move to the next level. From what I can tell, jiu jitsu is a lot more clear cut than other martial arts where you honestly have no real idea why you've progressed from one level to the next or what the difference is between one belt and another. Jiu jitsu requires you to perform against an opponent or with a partner on a regular basis. It can't be faked. You aren't swinging at air. You have a live person struggling with you, sometimes as an obstacle to be conquered and other times as a stepping stone to reach a greater height.

I found out that purple belt's name, finally. The one that I felt was out of line with me when we first met. He's a brown belt now and up until very recently I'd found just about every excuse I could imagine to avoid dealing with my negative feelings towards him. His name is Nathan; a large, powerful man with an incredible amount of skill in the jiu jitsu game. He's approximately my age and has a number of medals under his belt from various competitions. I happened to express some of my frustration to a mutual friend, Nick C. I think he was legitimately confused by the animosity because he knew us both and thought we were both nice guys. With hopes of clearing up the misunderstanding, he mentioned the issue to Nathan.

As one might think, he had no idea that there was a problem at all. We travel in different circles at the gym – him, mornings and me, evenings. So our interaction since that first encounter was very limited. One of those flashpoint moments was about to happen, though I was unaware of it at the time.

Nathan approaches me at the gym and the first thought through my head is "Yep, Nick said something." He grips my hand firmly and introduces himself and tells me that he's seen me a lot at the gym, validating my progress and effort along the way. Looking me squarely in the eye, he asks me if he has given offense and I explain how I feel. That's something new. In the past, I would have hemmed and hawed, withdrawn, or straight out lied. It feels good to express to him that I thought he had acted somewhat elitist and at the very least had hurt my feelings at a time when it could have changed whether or not I continued at the gym.

Nathan's response is something that I will never forget. He apologized, first and foremost, for the misunderstanding. It wasn't his intent to make me feel that way. In general, he says, he avoids rolling with white belts because they haven't developed enough control to avoid injuring themselves or others. I think back to my numerous injuries (ribs, hips, ankles, knees, elbows) and realize that they've all come from rolling with other white belts. I've never been hurt by a higher belt. He tells me that he'd like to roll with me more often because he's seen my progress and can tell that my game has developed a lot. I am flabbergasted. This guy isn't elitist. He's smart. We talk about longevity in the sport and something he calls 'flow rolling'. No submissions, just reading feeds and moving with your partner trying to recognize opportunities.

I recognize this opportunity. Personal growth has laid itself out right in front of me. I take Nathan up on his offer to roll. I have a blast, even though it is really obvious that he is light years ahead of me in the skill department. That means so little in the big picture. Every 'loss' is a learning experience. I have definitely learned something important. Judgment is best saved for when you've had the chance to read the whole book. The cover doesn't always show what's inside.

Open:

I feel it slipping away. There is an opportunity that I am about to miss if I don't take this risk. My life may be no better or worse in the long run if I don't pursue it, but every fiber of my being is telling me that I need to be persistent; if I stay inside my comfortable little box then I might miss out on something great.

Competing in the adult division is something that I've been avoiding. I'm 37 years old and there are times when my body reminds me of that in a loud and violent way. So far I have held my own and at times excelled in my own age division, but I feel that if I don't at least try to push myself then I will always be asking myself 'What if?' That is a question I want to avoid from here on out. The Oregon Open Adult Lightweight division just picked up a crusty, yet game, 'older' gentleman. Oh yeah, I dropped another five pounds to boot. I'm starting to think my natural body weight is somewhere between 155 and 160.

Liz has thrown up a roadblock to my efforts towards pursuing a relationship. It is painfully obvious that she feels drawn to me in the same way that I am pulled towards her, but there is something she isn't telling me; maybe she feels like she can't tell me. I resolve to give it at least one more try. The fact is I've never met anyone like her. She inspires and motivates me. Just by being herself.

It has been less than a week since Nationals, but physically I am feeling on top of my game. The Open is not just the first time that I'll be competing in the adult division, but also the first time that my team will be competing as Ribeiro-Lovato NW. This is significant because it represents many of the local gyms that would normally compete separately coming together as an association. I find it personally exciting because it makes it that much easier to network and get to know more people. The guys from Seaside and Salem are a great crew and add a lot to the already fantastic Five Rings flavor. We have a sea of yellow and black in the stands thanks to the new T-shirts we're all sporting.

This is new territory for me. It has never been a habit of mine to persist once rejected. I always felt that it came down to respect for the other person's wishes. This scenario is playing out differently; I think mostly because I am a different person. I recognize several things that are as clear to me as the moon on a cloudless winter's night: A) I am already infatuated to the nth degree, B) If I just let things drop then the most likely outcome is that we both continue on our merry way, and C) That spark between us burns in my dreams. I ask her to talk with me and to my surprise I lay everything in my heart out honestly. She is taken aback and needs time to think.

I have three matches today. They all end up looking and feeling about the same. It's not that I perform poorly. I end up taking home bronze by winning the first two matches. The difficulty I have is that my game seems somewhat unimaginative and ineffective today. My sweeps get me the points I need to win, but I have an incredibly hard time passing guard and maintaining cross sides. In the final match, my penchant for leaving my arms hanging away from my body gets me caught in a triangle. I was up 2 to 0 with very little time left on the clock. Reminiscent of my finals match at Nationals. Overall, I feel vindicated because I showed that I can compete with the 'young bucks' and do more than hold my own, but I also recognize that I have a lot to work on. I can't wait to get back to training!

The message I am currently reading from Liz has set me on fire. I am struggling with her admission of deception, yet excited beyond excitement by her willingness to give us a chance. This exceptional being sees something in me that I have only just begun to see in myself and I am literally dancing at the prospects the future holds. More reinforcement for persistent pursuit of what you want in life. I don't remember any of the classic romances starting with someone giving up!

Whirlwind:

I've heard it said that when it rains, it pours. My life at the moment is flooding. Rather than let it overwhelm me and pull me under, I build a raft so that I can enjoy every moment. My writing: the journal, the blog, the novel – these all help me focus the lens and appreciate all of the stimulation going on right now. It occurs to me that I am happier than I have been in a very long time.

My jiu jitsu community definitely keeps me on my toes. My conversations with Eric and Nick B. force me to constantly evaluate my progress in the realm of personal development and relationships. To have consistent access to feedback on my emotions is helping me to stay more even-keeled, rather than careening from highs to lows and slamming into trauma on either end of the spectrum.

Eric's Halloween bash is a blast. I go as Clay Guida (my favorite UFC fighter). A big crew shows up and for the first time since I was a teenager I spend the holiday completely sober. In fact, this is my one year sobriety anniversary. It is hard for me to believe that 365 days ago I was drooling in a chair in the drunk tank in downtown Portland, wondering how the hell I had gotten there. My memory is still somewhat hazy about it all, but it is with the deepest sense of respect that I recognize the progress that I have made.

Today I am able to feel a modicum of control over my life. If external forces cause upheaval, I have a support network to help me deal with it. I will never say that I've conquered my addictions. They are always lingering in the background. I will say that my addictions and I have come to terms with each other. I agree not to indulge in them and they agree not to take over my life. I keep them at bay with a healthy routine and a good diet.

Every once in a while I wonder when I am going to get my blue belt. I feel like I've covered the bases as far as learning the positions and pathways. I'm getting a lot of mat time and competition experience. I understand that there are other components to being promoted, even if I am not always able to identify exactly what they are yet. The green belt crew (there are 8 or 9 of us altogether at the moment) seems primed to make the leap. I resolve to worry less about it and focus on honing my game and filling in the existing gaps. I still have plenty more to learn.

The next Revolution tournament is coming up in early November. I can't wait for another opportunity to compete in the adult division and show what I can do. Pan Ams are further down the road, but it is never too early to start preparing. I take a moment to savor the opportunities and enjoy the place that I've come to. Lots of reasons to smile.

Reorientation:

I head in to a midday class at Five Rings expecting my regular session. Coach Greg is out sick today, so Coach Tom greets me as I walk onto the mat. I look around to discover that I am the only student present. It takes me a moment, but I soon realize that I'm about to get a private session with my gym's head coach. We get right down to it. Coach has me show him my game plan for the Revolution. Not much has changed since the Oregon Open. Slide guard, look for an opening for a triangle, arm bar, or omaplata.

Coach helps me focus in on a quicker and smoother triangle attack immediately from the slide. There are key points of tension and relaxation that I hadn't considered that tighten up the submission significantly. I drill this extensively and start to feel very comfortable with it. We also work on a scissor sweep and a knee block that has been somewhat effective for me in the past. Finally, I get to spend some time on what I consider my biggest weakness – guard passing. I cannot stress how valuable this one on one instruction feels. My confidence is soaring heading into the tournament.

Liz and I wake up early to head up to Bonney Lake. Normally I would try to arrive the night before, but I feel good about the amount of time that I have before I have to compete. Several of my teammates are also competing today. Liz is recovering from her victory in her first mixed martial arts fight last weekend, so has rightfully earned a break from competition. It was awesome to be able to support her during her battle and it feels equally good to have her by my side for mine. I've rehearsed my game plan many times, both on the mat and in my head and I feel ready to step on the mat.

The blue belts are competing first and Coach Tom is coaching the juniors in another room, so I jump in to help out my team by assisting one of our top blues, Kevin. He's affectionately known at the gym as the 'Yeah, he should be purple' guy. Outstanding body awareness and technical skills make the fact that he's only 19 all the more surprising. It's fun to take on the coaching role, even if all I'm really doing is shouting the time left and helping him warm up. He wins gold in his division!

The time for my match is quickly approaching. I note that my opponent is also a four-stripe white. I'm excited for a good match! We bow onto the mat and touch hands. I hesitate momentarily, trying to get a feel for his game. He takes advantage and slides guard straight into a triangle attempt. The thought briefly enters my mind that this guy is attacking me with my own strengths. I fend off the triangle only to have him transition into an arm bar. I am stronger than my opponent, and I defend well. I've got him stacked and try to pull my arm out. As I do, he bucks his hips into my elbow and before I know it I am in an extremely dark position. Sprawled out, arm extended, his hips driving at an odd angle into the side of my limb. I literally hear the meat of my arm tear and pop, but adrenaline and pride keep me from tapping. I pay the price when the bones start to grind together. I curse, tap, and go limp as my opponent releases me. I struggle to my feet, momentarily humiliated. The match has only lasted about two and a half minutes. My arm is definitely injured. Not hurt. Injured.

Anger and frustration are not emotions that I deal with well. The pain is secondary, but I am not handling the loss well. This is my first experience with losing in the first round and I do NOT like the feeling. It is hard to focus on the positive. I look at Coach Tom and remember the grace with which he accepted his losses at Nationals. I try to balance my emotions with that sentiment and am partially successful. The medic says at the very least that I've strained the ligaments on the inside of my elbow joint and that I need to ice and elevate it sooner than later. He recommends a visit to a physician and a minimum of two weeks off the mat. Pretty much a nightmare, from my perspective.

Liz gets the worst of it. The trip back to Portland progresses from sobs to sullenness to acceptance. She helps me to understand that the loss is nothing if I learned something from it. My biggest mistake was allowing my pride to put myself in a position for injury. Brazilian jiu jitsu is a pretty simple sport to avoid being injured in. Tapping is the secret. I have to ask myself, was it worth it? Was the small possibility that I was going to escape a deeply sunk in arm bar worth my ripped muscle? The answer is an unequivocal 'No'. I know that the next couple of weeks are going to be difficult. I just hope that I can use this experience to grow and not let it drag me down. Despite all of my preparation and confidence, this reminds me that life is unpredictable at times. Time to take a look in the mirror and decide why I am doing this and how much it is worth to me.

Recognition:

The reflection that stares back at me in the mirror reminds me that the Dan VanDetta I was once so familiar with is gone. Physically, it is easy to see the changes. I am over forty pounds lighter than I was one year ago. Muscle has replaced fat. I swear that my hair is even less grey than it used to be. It is the person I see behind my eyes, however, that has evolved into something most drastically new. There is a confidence there that was missing before. A belief that within me exists the capacity to achieve anything I set my mind to. I can still see insecurity fluttering around the periphery, but the control it once had is most assuredly gone.

I credit the art of jiu jitsu. The rhythm of training and competition, along with the camaraderie of being part of a team, has helped me discover the person that I always longed to be. Strong in mind and body, a person of integrity. The routine of being on the mat every day has awakened an appreciation for discipline and steady effort. The excitement and variety of competition reveal the wonder and passion I'd thought I had lost forever. The spirit of *ossu* has gradually, unerringly, sometimes even violently penetrated my being until the transformation is almost complete. This is NOT the result of some external, uncontrollable force. It is directly connected to the environment and people I have surrounded myself with.

The social and professional opportunities have been boundless. I have to give immense credit to the amazing people that I have had the pleasure of becoming friends, colleagues, and in one instance something more with.

Coaching has let me rediscover the joy I find in teaching. The juniors' class is an abundance of enthusiasm and I carry their energy even when we aren't together. The college students are like sponges, soaking up new information as fast as we can impart it. The adults in BJJ 1 overcome obstacles as daunting as the ones I had to face and then some. The process is a reminder of where I was and how far I've come. I feel really good about sharing what I have learned.

The friendships that developed in the last year help me to understand what I had been truly missing in the past. The laughter, shared confidences, and spectacular memories are intangible quantities that are priceless to me. Above all these is the presence of an emotional backboard. I am not sane, by the literal definition of the word. My friends allow my craziness to flow, receive it, and bounce it back to me in comforting terms that make sense in the world. I cannot express how valuable this is. I have also experienced the joy of being the person that others turn to for an opinion, advice, or just an open mind. That hasn't happened in a very long time.

I thought my heart was closed. Not dead, but barely breathing. Well protected in the fortress I had built around it. I was comfortable with the simplicity of focusing on myself; I wanted nothing more than to walk the pathway by myself. Friends were fine. Their paths and mine could intersect, but ultimately my road was going to have my footprints on it and mine alone. Perhaps the most surprising part of how my mind has changed is the metamorphosis in this area. The mortar of pain and insecurity has crumbled. The bricks of infidelity, addiction, and dishonesty have fallen. The feeling of building a relationship the 'right' way, if there is such a thing, is so consistently refreshing that I am almost overwhelmed by it on a daily basis. Communication, trust, honesty, integrity, love. Wow.

I stare into the mirror and recognize the effort that it has taken to get to this point. The effort of a community. Hours of instruction, training, mat time, miles on the road, listening, sharing, "extreme hugging", challenging, failing, succeeding, laughing, watching, doing, competing, cooperating, risking, and loving have gone into creating what I see before me. I recognize and resolve to never slow down, never give up, and never take for granted. I will always remember where I was and what it took for me to get here.

Reminiscence:

I look up into my mother's face as she whispers to me that everything is going to be fine. "You can take one toy, Danny, quickly then go to the truck with your brothers." I trust her, but it's dark and cold outside. "Where going?" my three-year-old brain stumbles to make connections. "Somewhere safe, away from here," replies Darryll, my oldest brother. As the tailgate shuts on the little green Toyota truck, the image of the only home I've ever known is burned into my memory. The beloved pets, the yard that I played in daily, and the father that caused so much pain left behind.

When I was a young boy, my mother took my brothers and me from our home to escape the abuses of my biological father. She left us with her parents not too long after that. My grandparents tried their best to raise another set of kids, but three rambunctious boys must have been a serious challenge more often than not. They provided food, shelter, and clothing. They supported us in our academic and extracurricular endeavors. My grandparents were amazing people. Despite this fact, I developed some serious abandonment issues that have impacted me throughout my life.

Self-reliance is a valuable tool that jiu jitsu has helped me to develop. I can draw on the resources of my community to help me achieve my goals, but ultimately when I step on the mat I have to rely on my strength, speed, conditioning, and training to perform and do the things that I want to do. Learning to relax in stressful situations and to examine the successes and taps in meaningful ways has gone a long way in helping me to become more secure in my ability to manage the real world. There is no doubt that it is still a struggle. I find myself falling into some familiar traps from time to time. My ability to get out of those traps has most assuredly improved, however.

I honestly can't remember the last time I had a birthday party. I've celebrated in small ways or completely ignored the passing of the year or become utterly depressed that no one else seemed to care. This year turns out to be a little different. Liz and I are supposed to get together for a quiet dinner, so I head over to her place. As I walk in, the shouts of 'Surprise!' take me completely off guard. I get lightheaded and can't stop the smile from leaping to my face. A large part of my community has showed up to help me celebrate – the Dorsetts, Nick B., Andreas and Tracy, Noah, Robert and Louisa, Nick M., Gabe... I even get to meet Liz's grandparents. The food is delicious and the conversation is great. Liz organized the whole thing. I am completely blown away.

My life is so different. The positive energy that I am putting into the world seems to be coming back to me with so much power. I am not grinding out my days. Passion is still my guiding force, but it is tempered by intelligent effort. The rewards are tangible and easily acknowledged. I know now that even if everyone that I love and care for were somehow removed from my life I would be okay. I could fall back on the rock that I've become for myself. I believe in me; I am my own best friend. I do not have to worry about being abandoned or left behind.

By the same token, I have gained a huge appreciation for the special bonds and relationships that have formed in my life. The ability to recognize special people and foster friendships with them is something not to be taken lightly. Surrounding myself with positive, passionate people has been the smartest change I've made. I've come to understand that we, as human beings, feed off the energy of those around us. It can motivate us to great achievements if it is positively directed, or it can drag us down if it is negative.

The foundation has been laid. The framework is in place. The scaffolding is set. I feel confident that I am ready to start putting the finishing touches on the life I've been building. It feels pretty damn good.

Courage:

People seem to handle the complexities of life with varying degrees of success. Some are able to handle work, family, friends, and finances with ease while others struggle to regulate even the simplest of personal issues. The brief time I've spent in this particular existence has shown me that the key to my happiness lies in recognizing where my limits are and continually pushing those boundaries (albeit with varying degrees of pressure, as needed). Growth is important. Knowing when I'm overloaded or stagnating is, too.

I've painstakingly examined and adjusted the balance of simplicity and complexity in my life on an almost daily basis. Sometimes it is very obvious – like when I feel like I am overtraining at the gym, I take some time off. If I feel like I'm sitting in front of the TV or computer for too long I go out for a run. Those come pretty easily to me now, even if they didn't in the past. There are other, more instinctual choices that I make as well. Investments of my time and effort into people that may need my help require some intuitive analysis. Reactions to the unexpected or uncontrollable, particularly in relationships, need to be tempered by reason and experienced with emotion.

Fear is still my greatest enemy. It comes in all flavors. Insecurity, anxiety, panic, dread – all of them dance in my subconscious, threatening to steal the progress I've made. As I've added more complexity to my life the fear gets harder to keep at bay. I have to use the tools I've developed to combat it. Confidence, reliance, belief, and trust - these are my allies. I know that if I stay true to the path I've chosen then I can continue to be happy, achieve my goals, and find fulfillment in my life.

Thanksgiving is an interesting time for me. I've had so many different experiences at this time of year. Last year, for instance, was wonderful. I spent the day with my brother's family and his in-laws. It was my first sober holiday, and I was surrounded by supportive, loving people. I had a lot to be thankful for. The fact that I was still breathing, for one. On the other end of the spectrum, I've suffered through nightmarish 'Jerry Springer' style family blowouts with all the ridiculous drama those entail. Even worse, at times, were the Thanksgivings eating out at a restaurant, alone. This year I spend it with my girlfriend, Liz, and her family. They are warm and welcoming and I am reminded of all the things I have to express gratitude for. There is good food, great conversation, and lots of laughs.

Every day is a new day, filled with possibility. Whether I am met with joy or disappointment, laughter or sadness I know that I am alive and that I am powerful beyond measure. I have not conquered fear, but I am much more willing to face it. I have heard it said that the difference between courage and stupidity is that in order to be brave you must be aware of the danger and choose to act anyhow. Idiocy is born of ignorance. I have witnessed many forms of courage. Standing up for what you believe to be right, in the face of peer pressure. Honesty, even when the consequence is severe loss. Pursuing future dreams that could benefit many others at the expense of current ones that impact primarily you. I push myself to own this kind of courage.

Citizenship:

Coach Tom asks Liz and me to make sure that we show up to tournament rounds because some of our peers are getting promoted. He assures us that we're on the radar, too, but because of our recent injuries we'll just be there to support and initiate our teammates. There are quite a few people 'on deck' for promotion and it's exciting to be a part of that process for them. I feel a brief moment of disappointment that I'm not getting my blue belt, but I stifle it quickly. My time will come.

Life is solid right now. There are moments of extreme joy and sadness, but these are not the turning points that they used to be. I appreciate them for what they are. What I've come to recognize is that the larger spectrum of ups and downs contains an incredible rainbow of experience. Sometimes I find the most happiness in the routine of a 'normal' day. Training, working, writing... the intangibles of consistent effort are something that I have come to value a great deal. On the other hand, the variety of managing relationships and enjoying the passions of my friends keeps life interesting. It's a balancing act of personal growth and I love every second.

Tuesday night comes quickly and Five Rings is packed. I look around the room and see the familiar faces of friends and training partners; these are my compatriots on my journey. I see Jonathan, Ziggy, and Evan. Those teenagers have been sitting on the edge of blue for a while now and from my experiences rolling with them it wouldn't surprise me in the slightest if they got promoted tonight. Noah is another one – a former wrestler who has won a couple of tournaments at the white belt level and is quite simply, a monster. Great body awareness, particularly considering he's right around 250 lbs.

We start off with some closed guard positional sparring and I look for an opportunity to roll with the guys that will be getting their blue belts. Five Rings doesn't test like some academies do, but there is a bit of a gauntlet to pass before getting promoted. For ninety minutes you are pushed to your physical limits by your coaches and fellow jiu jitsu practitioners. All of the people I think might be getting promoted are taken, so Robert and I pair up. We get after it and he just works me. My neck is feeling the punishment from the repeated bow and arrow chokes, for sure. The next round I hook in with Toby, one of our judo takedown instructors. I do a little better, getting a sweep and some half guard time in. I can tell it is going to be an interesting evening. Everyone is on their game.

As time progresses, I notice a pattern. Louie brings his 'A' level when we roll. Coach Greg hits me with three or four chokes and even yells at me to keep working when my energy starts to flag. This strikes me as a little unusual because he normally gives me some room to work when we roll. Every time I head for one of my regular training partners I get snagged by an upper belt. The rounds are also coming fast and furious so I don't get a chance to get off the mat for a break, either. More submissions, more domination, more encouragement to work harder. I am feeling the workout tonight!

Sweat pours down my face and my breathing is labored, to say the least. I get Toby again for what Coach Tom likes to call 'Oh Shucks' drills. We start with our partner in the position we find most challenging – for many, it is mount bottom or back with hooks. I have Toby start in cross sides because I've been struggling with that position a lot lately. Again, he brings it to me. I have very little room and less energy to try to escape. He holds me down as cheering starts erupting from around me. At this point I've figured out that something isn't exactly as I was told, but I'm so tired that it hasn't clicked in yet. More cheers and I hear Coach say that the best way to celebrate promotions is to keep rolling. I try my hardest.

After what seems like an eternity, Toby rolls me over and I try to pass his guard. I feel something hook around my waist from behind. Toby catches my eye and smiles. I drop to my knees as I realize what is happening and bury my face in my hands. I see flashes of fresh blue material as I peek out from between my fingers. I am so exhausted physically and now my emotions take a huge hit. I have worked hard and for many hours to reach this landmark. I can't hold back the tears.

In this moment, the changes in my life are highlighted. It is almost exactly a year since I started down my new path of discovery and challenges. My capacity for appreciating the world that I exist in has increased exponentially. I savor every ounce of sweat and blood that it has taken to get here. I recognize each person that has helped along the way, and give credit where it is due. My fears and insecurities have faded to the background, replaced by confidence and purpose.

I finally rise to my feet and stumble around the mat, accepting congratulations and offering them to the others that were promoted with me. I'd predicted it fairly well – Noah, Ziggy, Evan, and Jonathan all got their blue. From out of the corner of my eye I spot a streak of blonde hustling towards me. I open my arms wide and embrace Liz – the blue around her waist matches her eyes. This is a moment I will never forget for the rest of my life.

This is not an end, but a beginning. The year of training has shown me how much I still have to learn and how much room there is for growth. I look forward to improving my jiu jitsu and helping others to do the same through taking on more coaching opportunities. I will continue to compete as long as my body allows me to do so. I cannot express appropriately the amount of gratitude that I have for the Five Rings community – my coaches, teammates, training partners, and friends that have walked every step of this journey with me.

Afterword:

My footsteps continue to walk along the path of health and wellness. Growth and balance are my priorities these days. I've learned to manage my life and cope with the stress that comes along with being a part of human society. If even one of you found some inspiration, motivation, or hope from reading this story then it was worth the time and effort that went into creating it.

When I stop to think about how much I have gained from being a part of the Five Rings community, I am overwhelmed by the feelings of gratitude in my heart. My coaches – Tom, Eric, Nick, Aaron, and Greg – have guided me with precision and care. They are exceptional models of great instructors and I hope that all of you that participate in the sport are lucky enough to have people like them to help you.

I am currently a blue belt at the time this missive is being published. Recently, I competed in my first tournament at this level and won a gold medal. I also competed at the Pan Am tournament and lost in the first round. The roller coaster continues to thrill me and I am working diligently to keep improving my game and my life.

I deeply appreciate any feedback you might have and love to hear about how my words may have impacted you. I can be reached online at http://rivengard.blogspot.com . I look forward to reading your stories!

Acknowledgements:

I am very grateful to the following people for allowing me to use their images and/or names in this blog:

Eric Dorsett, Tom Oberhue, Nick Burke, Jessica Sexton, Nathan Jeffers, Nick Childs, Andreas Correa, Robert Wolfe, Louisa Bruschi, Justin Lau, Noah Gordon, Saulo Ribeiro, Tracy Correa, Hixon Dorsett, Chloe Dorsett, Gabe Kniffin, Will Acton, Xavier Smith, select members of the graduating class of Granville High School '91, Paula Genier, Megan Long, Sean Cavanagh, Bob Ives, David Lord, Troy Zimmerman, Steve Longo, Seton Seto, Larry Reynolds, Bruce McMinn, Evan Peters, Ziggy Kotchetkev, Jonathan Davidson, Nick Marvin, Kevin Dadik, Brian House, Toby Presnell, Matt Phongsavanh and anyone else whose name or image appears within.

 I offer a special thank you to Liz Tracy for her understanding and support of this and all of my efforts. Much love.

12688676R00054

Made in the USA
Charleston, SC
21 May 2012